T0330661

Network Industries

"The important roles networks play in economics, politics, business, sociology, and virtually everything humans engage in has become increasingly recognized, but we really understand little of the detail of individual networks, let alone their dynamics and interactions. This short book fills a major gap by providing a very carefully thought through and clear introduction to what we do know about network industries, essentially those activities that allow us to move, to transport goods, and to communicate."

Kenneth Button, *George Mason University, USA*

"Drawing on both interdisciplinary theory and contemporary practice, Professor Finger offers an essential, insightful, and comprehensive treatment of network and utility industries – including their comparative historical development and relationship to the regulatory state as well as the institutional implications of today's transformative technologies."

Janice Beecher, *Michigan State University, USA*

The unique challenges associated with understanding network industries requires insights from a range of disciplinary perspectives, namely economics, engineering, law, and political science. This book analyzes the de- and re-regulation of the network industries and the regulatory challenges these industries will face in the future.

Network industries are characterized by economics that entail limiting effects on competition and market creation, and the book highlights the drivers behind their liberalization as well as the inherent need for regulation as liberalization unfolds. By way of an historical approach, the author offers insights into the distinctive approaches between Europe and North America in the past whilst also presenting the pervasive role digitalization increasingly comes to play.

A concise overview of the state of thinking about the network industries, this book will be vital reading for researchers, advanced students and practitioners.

Matthias Finger is Swiss Post Chair in Management of Network Industries at the Swiss Federal Institute of Technology in Lausanne, Switzerland.

State of the Art in Business Research
Edited by Professor Geoffrey Wood

Recent advances in theory, methods and applied knowledge (alongside structural changes in the global economic ecosystem) have presented researchers with challenges in seeking to stay abreast of their fields and navigate new scholarly terrains.

State of the Art in Business Research presents shortform books which provide an expert map to guide readers through new and rapidly evolving areas of research. Each title will provide an overview of the area, a guide to the key literature and theories, and time-saving summaries of how theory interacts with practice.

As a collection, these books provide a library of theoretical and conceptual insights, and exposure to novel research tools and applied knowledge, that aid and facilitate in defining the state of the art as a foundation stone for a new generation of research.

Mergers and Acquisitions
A Research Overview
David R. King, Florian Bauer and Svante Schriber

Strategic Human Resource Management
A Research Overview
John Storey, Dave Ulrich and Patrick M. Wright

Flexible Working in Organizations
A Research Overview
Clare Kelliher and Lilian M. de Menezes

Network Industries
A Research Overview
Matthias Finger

For more information about this series, please visit: www.routledge.com/State-of-the-Art-in-Business-Research/book-series/START

Network Industries

A Research Overview

Matthias Finger

Routledge
Taylor & Francis Group

LONDON AND NEW YORK

First published 2020
by Routledge
2 Park Square, Milton Park, Abingdon, Oxon OX14 4RN

and by Routledge
52 Vanderbilt Avenue, New York, NY 10017

Routledge is an imprint of the Taylor & Francis Group, an informa business

© 2020 Matthias Finger

British Library Cataloguing-in-Publication Data
A catalogue record for this book is available from the British Library

Library of Congress Cataloging-in-Publication Data
A catalog record for this book has been requested

ISBN: 978-1-138-32693-4 (hbk)
ISBN: 978-0-429-44956-7 (ebk)

Typeset in Times New Roman
by Apex CoVantage, LLC

Contents

Introduction

This book introduces network industries in general and the main network industries – in the areas of communications, transport, and energy – in particular. It focuses on their liberalization as well as on their regulation, considering that network industries are a very particular type of industry, which always have been and always will be regulated in one way or another. Consequently, this book explains how network industry liberalization took place and how network industry re-regulation gradually came into place.

As such, this book is resolutely interdisciplinary. Even though I am, originally, a political scientist, the past almost 20 years of my academic career have been spent in an engineering environment, and this environment has provided the most valuable lesson for me: network industries are, first of all, technology based and technology shaped. Even if we try to apply to them political and, increasingly, economic considerations and sometimes recipes, technology remains their key feature, no matter how stubborn the politician or economist. Furthermore, infrastructures – this word being used synonymously with network industries when not explicitly specified otherwise – cost a lot of money and generally are built to last for quite some time, and thus they generate "sunk costs" and create lock-ins, as well as all kinds of economic and social effects. A historical perspective is thus also in order.

As the editor-in-chief of the journal *Competition and Regulation in Network Industries* and the co-editor-in-chief of two handbooks on the de- and re-regulation of these industries (Finger and Künneke, 2011; Finger and Jaag, 2015), I have acquired not only an interdisciplinary but also a global understanding of what is occurring in the various network industries. I would like to share this knowledge with my readers.

Finally, the book links theory and practice. It is born out of my academic work but mostly out of my experience. As a regulator, I have had the quite unique opportunity of being a member of the Swiss railway regulatory authority for 12 years as well as of the Swiss electricity market regulatory authority for another 12 years. And as a practically minded academic, I have been fortunate to be able to witness and actively accompany the 20 most interesting years of network industry de- and re-regulation. As a director at the Florence School of Regulation since 2010, I have furthermore had a unique chance to work directly with the European Commission, in particular with the Directorate General in charge of transport and mobility (DG MOVE). The European Commission is, without a doubt, the major actor in matters of network industries' de- and re-regulation since the 1990s. I have also been fortunate to meet and at times to work with particularly important regulators and academics (sometimes combining both roles) who have shaped the evolution of the different network industries through their regulation. Finally, I have been the holder of a sponsored chair since 2002, namely the Swiss Post Chair in Management of Network Industries. Thanks to this function, I have had the rare opportunity to directly experience how regulation affects firm behavior and firm strategy. I am truly indebted to the Swiss Post for having offered me such a rich learning environment. During my tenure at École Polytechnique Fédérale Lausanne (EPFL), I have supervised over 30 PhD students who, with almost no exception, have conducted their research while working part-time either in regulated firms or in regulatory authorities, this across all network industries. I have learned a lot from them and thank them all for having helped me to go deeper in certain issues than I could have done alone.

As my professional career is slowly coming to an end, I seize this opportunity to look back, sometimes critically, at how network industry liberalization and re-regulation has unfolded since the 1990s, when it all began. But I feel that network industries are also somewhat at a crossroads: if the past 25 to 30 years were characterized by their de- and re-regulation, something profoundly new is starting to affect the various network industries recently, namely digitalization. It is undeniable that in the past five to ten years, the various network industries – starting with telecommunications, followed by transport and most recently by energy – have been pervasively penetrated by information and communication technologies, with consequences yet to be fully understood.

This addition of digitalization leads, in my opinion, to the most dramatic changes in all the network industries since their inception, typically in the late 19th century. As a result, the network industries of the future may look very different from what they are today and from what they were in the past. Indeed, only time will tell whether pervasive digitalization will actually further the process of liberalization and competition, whether it will give rise to a new wave of regulation, or whether it will mean the end of competition altogether. At some point we will have to ask ourselves whether, in the future, these digital platforms are going to be the new network industries, replacing the traditional network industries of over 100 years. Therefore, at the end of this book, I discuss digitalization and the emergence of digital platforms as the new network industries (Chapter 11).

This book is structured as follows: in the first chapter, I explain why, at least in my mind, network industries are an intellectually interesting topic. Next, I present why they are and always will be regulated (Chapter 2). I show how network industry regulation is a profoundly political activity, even though the very aim of regulation is to somewhat shelter the different network industries from direct political intervention (Chapter 3). Chapter 4 presents and discusses regulatory authorities, which are probably the most radical institutional innovation since the creation of the modern nation state. Chapters 5 and 6 are devoted to the regulation of the remaining network industry monopolies, even after their liberalization, as well as to the attempts to create competition, nevertheless. Chapters 7 to 10 serve as short introductions to the main network industries (communications, transport, energy, and water), their liberalization, and their regulation. As stated previously, Chapter 11 as well as the conclusion examine new developments in network industries caused by digitalization and assess their future evolution.

This book is the result of my personal observations and active involvement in the various network industries. Consequently, references are limited to what I consider essential reading if one wants to acquire a quick, yet comprehensive, understanding of the topic.

1 Why are network industries interesting?

This chapter presents and explains why network industries constitute a relevant and interesting topic, both for academics and practitioners. For most of us, network industries became interesting in the context of their liberalization, as before that they were considered to be sleepy, state-owned monopolies. But network industries were, of course, interesting far before their liberalization, which remains unfinished and partial and has recently been overtaken by other public policy objectives, as we will see. Thus, the history of network industries can be divided into roughly three phases, namely the periods before, during, and beyond liberalization.

Before liberalization: state-owned enterprises

Why were network industries interesting before their liberalization? To make it simple, mainly because the main societal functions of the different industries were defined at that time, and most of these functions continue to be valid today. What has changed with liberalization is the way these functions are performed, or more precisely how these various network industries are organized and governed so that these functions can (or in some cases can no longer) be performed. But let us proceed historically.

Private origins

Before industrialization took hold in Europe during the second half of the 19th century, no network industries existed, only fragmented operations pertaining to communications, transport, energy, and water. The first such operations were probably courier services, which later became postal services. They were organized as concessions by those in power yet operated by private entrepreneurs linked cities and city states in medieval Europe. Railways emerged in a similar way during the second half of the 19th century, when private companies, granted permission by public authorities, built lines between cities where sufficient traffic could be generated to make a profit. Telecommunications, electricity, and water services emerged predominantly in cities around the same time period; that is, parallel to the early urbanization in Europe, the United States, and the European colonies. These services were not connected among themselves and only catered to paying customers, as most of the services were operated by private companies yet generally granted permission by local and sometimes national authorities.

Network integration: from private to public monopolies

As we have come to learn since, network industries are characterized by strong (economic) network effects: the more customers are connected to the network, the better it is for everybody, and a monopoly infrastructure is generally more efficient than fragmented and even competing "networks." This is particularly true in a period of infrastructure development, when corresponding investments (such as into rail, electricity, telecommunications, and water networks) are needed, as was the case during the rapid industrial development of the late 19th and the early 20th centuries and up to the 1970s. But such infrastructure monopolies do not necessarily need to be public, as one can see in the case of John Pierpont Morgan, the American financier, who understood early on how one could reap monopoly profits by investing into connecting scattered infrastructures, be it in telecommunications, railways, or electricity (Strouse, 1999). Yet the United States was and remains an exception worldwide, not least because of the country's federalist nature. In most other countries, and especially in Europe and the European colonies, the integration and the monopolization of the different network industries in public hands became a tool of nation building.

Indeed, there is more to public ownership than network effects, as the different network industries – in particular postal services, telecommunications (integrated with postal services into what became called "PTT" in all countries worldwide except the United States), railways, and electricity – were actively used by government as a means for national development, cohesion, control, and nation building more generally. And such nation building provided an additional justification – besides network effects leading to monopolization – for the nationalization of the different network industries during the late 19th and early 20th centuries in most industrialized countries. Thus, most network industries became public monopolies in the form of state-owned enterprises (SOEs).

Post and telecommunications (PTTs) were typically national public monopolies. As for railways and electricity, the status depended on the nature of the state: in the centralized countries, as is the case in the majority of the countries of the world, railways, roads, and later air transport, as well as electricity and later gas, became national public monopolies. In the federalist countries, rail and electricity turned into regional public monopolies. Publicly granted private ownership survived in some local network industries, such as water or public transport, yet only in some countries, such as, interestingly, in France. France, as we will see later, gave birth to the so-called "French model," also known as the PPP model (public-private partnership), a form of public control over privately operated local monopolies.

The SOE as the model provider of public (network) services

Thus was born the typical SOE as monopolistic provider of infrastructure services, most typically at the national but in the federalist countries also at the federal level. In the Latin-language-based European countries (France, Southern Europe), SOEs became known as public services providers if they were not flatly called "public services." At the local level and in the Anglo-Saxon context, these SOEs were called utilities or public utilities. In the German context (including Austria and Switzerland), several such utilities merged into so-called "Stadtwerke" (or urban utilities). What characterizes all these public enterprises is the fact that they provide infrastructure services – communications, transport, energy, and water – by way of a public monopoly on a given territory, typically the nation-state. While they can and do generate revenues, their mission is not merely commercial, as they simultaneously have to provide public services functions, such as national development; security, national, and social cohesion; employment; and many other political functions.

In short, while the economic rationale for the monopolization of the network industries lies in their network effects, the political rationale has stemmed from the process of nation building since the late 19th century and from active support for national economic and social development during a great part of the 20th century. The development of the SOEs was halted only when globalization started to show its consequences in the late 1980s.

The liberalization period (1980s–)

Liberalization of the network industries started in the late 1980s at a global scale. Whether it has ended or not is a matter of debate. However, what caused liberalization to begin with is clear, namely a combination of factors, all somewhat related to globalization. Besides the drivers of network industry liberalization, I will discuss, in this section, the two main approaches to liberalization: the United States (US)/World Bank (WB) and the European Union (EU) approaches. At the end of this section, I will come back to the

SOEs, which are particularly challenged by liberalization, challenges that makes the study of the network industries especially interesting.

The causes and drivers of liberalization

Liberalization has been triggered by at least three different forces – ideas (or ideologies), technology, and particular actors – all of which are also drivers of globalization. At an ideological level, neoliberalism has certainly been the most forceful driver. Neoliberalism comes in the form of an economic theory; that is, the belief that free and global markets not only lead to economic growth but simultaneously to social development and ultimately to world peace. In its most simplistic form, neoliberalism states that the freer the markets – that is, the less regulatory interventions – the better for economic growth, social development, and public welfare. Neoliberalism has been offered a significant boost by the demise of the Soviet empire and the fall of the Berlin Wall in 1989, all of which combined significantly accelerated world trade and economic globalization.

At a technological level, the early developments of information and communication technologies (ICTs) during the 1970s also significantly contributed to the economic globalization of the late 1980s. Indeed, the ICTs, together with the emerging global Internet, significantly accelerated the global exchange of information as well as global financial transactions. This in turn favored financial globalization and foreign direct investments (FDIs). Furthermore, progress in transport technologies, combined with FDI and the Internet, led to the globalization of "just-in-time" production (and consumption).

At an institutional level, neoliberal globalization was actively pushed by concrete actors. At the global level, this was mostly the WB and the International Monetary Fund (IMF), which in turn reflected the US government's and the transnational corporations' (TNCs') global geopolitical and financial ambitions. At the European level, a particular form of neoliberal approach was pushed by the EU's and more specifically the European Commission's (EC's) ambition to create a single European market.

The World Bank approach to liberalization: privatization

I simplistically equate privatization with the "World Bank approach" to liberalization simply because the World Bank pushed privatization most prominently throughout the 1980s. Yet privatization was also promoted by many other actors, notably the IMF, Margaret Thatcher, and the New Zealand and Chilean governments. All were strongly inspired by neoliberal economic thinking. But beyond ideology, privatization also responds to the need to attract private investment into infrastructure or simply to the need by some governments to pay off their previously accumulated debt.

The argument in favor of privatization claims that privately owned and managed companies will be more efficient and more innovative than government-owned and -managed ones. This statement is not necessarily wrong, though it is quite simplistic, as it ignores the broader industry context. In the context of the network industries, the SOEs were mostly monopolies, and privatization simply led to replacing public monopolies with private ones, which, by the way, is the reason why the governments could attract private investors. Consequently, privatization and the WB approach generally did not lead to competition, lower prices, and innovation; in the end, the private monopolies had to be regulated, and competition still had to be created. This is where the EU approach comes in.

The EU approach to liberalization: de- and re-regulation

I equate de- and re-regulation with the "EU approach" to liberalization simply because the EU – and more precisely the EC – created it during the 1990s and has been perfecting it ever since. Today, this EU approach has become *the* model of network industry liberalization. It has become de facto the only intellectually sound approach to the liberalization of the network industries, yet it exists at various levels of perfection in different parts of the world. Most of this book will therefore be about the EU approach.

In its origin in the early 1990s, this EU approach responded to an EU problem, if not *the* EU problem: namely Europe's lack of political integration. Creating an internal market by way of de- and re-regulating the network industries (and some other) industries was considered to be the most appropriate means to create a more politically integrated Europe. Majone has, in my view, rightly called this approach "Regulatory Europe," as it basically reflects the EU's aspiration to become something like a nation-state (Majone, 2005). Yet, since the EU does not own anything (as nation-states typically do), its only means toward political integration is (state-backed and state-enforced) regulation.

The main argument and cornerstone of the EU approach to liberalization is "unbundling," another somewhat more sophisticated idea of neoliberal economics. Unbundling states that infrastructures should and actually can be neatly separated into two parts: what is and needs to stay monopolistic (and become regulated) and what can and should be exposed to competition (and could remain almost unregulated). This approach was declined in various more- or less-pure forms in the different, separate network industries, reflecting both the resistance to liberalization by the state-owned monopolies as well as the different network industries' technological specificities. Never, though, does the EU use nor advocate privatization, the main objective being a level playing field among economic actors, be they publicly or privately owned. Nevertheless, all SOEs were profoundly affected by this approach, as well as, of course, by privatization.

Implications to SOEs

These effects pertain simultaneously to the services SOEs used to provide, to their strategies, and to their relationship with their owners; that is, the governments who (used to) consider them as public policy tools. SOEs – privatized or not – had and still have to adapt to this new, more competitive environment.

A significant amount of literature addresses the behavior of large firms under regulation, showing, in particular, that these firms try to shape such regulation to their advantage, notably by way of so-called "non-market strategies" or, in plain language, "lobbying." Such considerations, of course, also apply to SOEs, which, indeed, try to lobby for their respective monopolies when exposed to competition. But in the case of the SOEs, things are more complicated, as the same SOEs also display a somewhat schizophrenic behavior, namely when it comes to advocating for deregulation abroad (so that they can enter deregulated markets) while advocating for strong regulation domestically (so as to profit from their monopoly positions as long as possible). Also, SOEs, if they are not privatized, are typically more strongly regulated than their competitors, something also called "asymmetric regulation," owing in particular to the fact that they are still the ones having to provide public services, something private competitors will not do. Consequently, SOEs try not only to expand internationally (where they are treated as competitors and thus more lightly regulated) but also to diversify into less or even non-regulated businesses.

In other words, network industries are not only interesting because of the industry dynamics resulting from liberalization but also because the traditional SOEs are undergoing profound changes and because their transformation processes turn out to be interesting in themselves, caught as they are between markets and government. Also, most of the SOEs, at least the ones in the network industries, are not (yet) privatized and thus continue to perform public service functions, which barely differ from the functions they performed when they were created to begin with. Indeed, they often still play a significant role in national and social development and cohesion. However, in the network industries that are fully liberalized with private operators – which so far is only the case for airlines and telecommunication operators in most countries – governments have to find other ways to provide such public service functions, which is, as we will see, another source of network industry regulation.

Liberalization, no matter how it was originally triggered (privatization or deregulation) and no matter how it is being regulated, has created significant dynamics in all the network industries and as such has affected the behavior of all the involved actors, be it SOEs (also called incumbents), new entrants, or governments in their roles as policy makers, owners, and regulators. And such dynamics pertain not only to competition and markets but increasingly also to technological developments and innovations. Yet liberalization – especially the EU approach of de- and re-regulation – was not prepared for such technological dynamics, focused as it was, and still is, on creating, maintaining, and perfecting (internal) markets. Nevertheless, the past ten years have given rise to numerous technological changes in the various network industries, as well as cross-sectoral technological innovations, namely when it comes to digitalization. And this raises the question of whether we are not witnessing a new, post-liberalization period, characterized by a much more profound transformation of the networks or even the creation of new, digital networks. And all this makes the network industries even more interesting.

After and beyond liberalization (2010–)

Originally network industries – both their liberalization and their regulation – was mainly interesting for economists. The regulation of the different network industries is still mostly about economics. Consequently, the major part of this book will be devoted to the economic approach to network industries' de- and re-regulation: competition has to be created and made workable. And this is the task of the so-called independent regulatory authorities (IRAs). In their job, they should be inspired by regulatory economic theory (see Chapter 2).

But because regulation is a legal activity, the network industries are also interesting for lawyers, be they competition-specific or sector-specific lawyers. In addition, network industry liberalization has raised fundamental questions about public service and public policy more generally, which makes them also interesting for political economists and political scientists. The challenges to the original SOEs also raised questions about public governance and made network industries, or at least these transforming SOEs, interesting for public management scholars. Each of these disciplines has its own specific view of network industries.

Yet the recent dynamics of the network industries, triggered by profound sector-specific technological developments but even more so by cross-cutting digitalization, has brought the role of engineering back into focus. The economic liberalization of the network industries has somewhat downplayed, if not flatly ignored, the fact that all the network industries – except perhaps for the early postal services – owe their very existence to engineers and engineering. And as I will argue throughout this book, it is illusionary to manage and to regulate the different network industries without a sound understanding of their underlying technologies. With pervasive digitalization, this becomes ever truer.

And such digitalization – especially its impacts upon the different network industries – raises a series of questions, most of which are not yet fully understood and can thus not be systematically treated in this book. For example, will digitalization accelerate or actually reverse liberalization of the network industries? If digitalization is accelerating liberalization, will this have to lead to profound changes in the way the network industries are being regulated? And how should the network industries be regulated in the age of their digitalization? Will digitalization itself have to be regulated? If yes, how?

Digitalization raises even more radical questions, such as whether digitalization transforms the traditional network industry services – such as transport, energy, and communication services – into simple "commodities," commercialized via digital platforms. In this case, would these platforms become the "new network industries," a sort of new infrastructure? Would they have to be regulated in the same way as the traditional infrastructures? Or not? Could they even be regulated, given their inherently global nature? In other words, network industries – old or new – remain dynamic and interesting. This is what this book is all about.

2 Why do network industries need regulation?

This chapter is devoted to the economic theory of regulation. The next chapter will present the practice of regulation as it has evolved over time, which has ended up, of course, being quite different from theory. However, it is still important to talk about the theory for two main reasons: first, economic theory has served as a key argument for deregulation to begin with, and this argument will be presented in the first two sections of this chapter. Second, economic theory also serves as a beacon against which practices of regulation should be assessed (Nicita and Belloc, 2016); that is, as a so-to-speak ideal type of regulation. Consequently, sections three and four will discuss the two prevailing approaches to network industries' regulation, namely network economics on the one hand and public goods theory on the other.

So, why liberalize to begin with? Welfare – the sum of consumer and producer surplus – is the normative criterion used by economists to promote markets as well as to determine whether markets work or not. Indeed, according to economic theory, welfare is maximized under perfect competition, meaning that consumers do not pay too much for their products and services and that producers do not earn too little to develop their business. In other words, the market, and not regulation, according to economists, creates the optimal level of welfare.

But the market does not always work perfectly, and thus some government intervention into this not perfectly working market may be justified. However, how much government intervention is ultimately necessary depends on the very assessment of why the market fails to begin with. Regardless of such an assessment, it is important to note that the ultimate purpose always is to optimize welfare. Government intervention into markets – or regulation in the case of network industries – is therefore always only a second-best solution, a substitute for the not perfectly working market. The ultimate goal, from an economic theory point of view, always is to make regulation obsolete or at least to reduce it to a minimum.

Why do markets fail?

What has to be regulated and how intrusive regulation ultimately is – into both markets and firms – depends on why markets are considered to fail. In economic theory, there are basically three reasons why markets can fail: monopoly, public goods, and information asymmetry. The first two are of particular concern when it comes to justifying regulating the network industries; they are discussed here. The third one is particularly relevant when it comes to assessing the costs of regulation and regulatory institutions. I will discuss this in Chapter 4.

- Monopoly – also called market dominance or market power – was and continues to be the main reason why the network industries must be liberalized to begin with, as monopolies do not maximize welfare. Paradoxically, monopoly is also the main reason why they still have to be regulated, even after their liberalization. Economists question whether infrastructure services cannot be treated just like any other service or commodity, whereby consumers can simply choose differentiated products and services from competing providers. This is of course a very simplistic view, but it inspired both the EU and the WB approaches to liberalization: while the EU wanted to create an internal market whereby all European citizen-consumers could choose among different infrastructure providers, the World Bank, on the other hand, wanted to facilitate market entry for infrastructure services companies. But it rapidly became clear during the process of their liberalization that infrastructure services were not exactly commodities like bananas and yogurt and that some monopolies or at least monopolistic bottlenecks would remain even after full liberalization. This situation is precisely why a more sophisticated argumentation regarding monopolies became necessary (see the next section of this chapter) and why ultimately a whole field of so-called regulatory economics emerged (see section three of this chapter entitled "From network economics to regulatory economics").
- Public goods, broadly speaking, are goods and services that would not spontaneously be offered by profit-seeking firms because it would difficult or impossible to make a profit. Yet they are considered necessary for society and even for the economy to function. In the case of infrastructure, one speaks here of the "foundational economy" (Foundational Economy Collective, 2018). Obviously, many infrastructure services are foundational; that is, they constitute a necessary condition for other economic activities to even exist. In other words, many infrastructures of a public goods nature would not be provided if it were not for government, or they would be provided only at high prices that

only some customer-citizens could afford, which in turn would be sub-optimal for society; that is, it would generate social equity problems or otherwise hamper the full potential of economic development. The societal need for such public goods and services was used to justify the public provision or even the public ownership of infrastructure services in the past. However, in the context of liberalization, when companies compete and no longer have monopolies that allow them to cross-subsidize non-lucrative services with lucrative ones, the question emerges as to what to do with public goods. Should they simply be sacrificed on the altar of liberalization, or is it possible to have public goods – and foundational infrastructures for that matter – even in the context of competition and profit-seeking operators (be they publicly or privately owned)? And this question led to the question of the regulatory environment that would have to be designed so that profit-seeking operators would still have incentives to provide public goods. This type of regulatory intervention will be discussed in the last section of this chapter.

The idea of liberalization was to overcome the market failures in the network industries. But market failures persisted after liberalization: some monopolies remained, and many public goods were no longer provided after liberalization. Consequently, state intervention was considered legitimate even for neoliberal economists. But instead of owning SOEs, public intervention now took the form of regulation. Consequently, economists came around: after having argued for liberalization, they were now also providing the theory for regulation, yet regulation that was seen as creating and perfecting the markets, at worst as a substitute for the market – a perverse argumentation. The remainder of this chapter presents the different types of argumentations economists use as to why and how to regulate the (halfway) liberalized network industries.

From monopolies to their liberalization to their regulation

The original idea of liberalization as put forward by neoliberal economists was quite simple, if not simplistic and even naïve: after an initial phase during which regulation was necessary to "kill the monopolists" by way of creating competition, markets would set in, and (sector-specific) regulation would no longer be necessary. Competition regulation would ultimately suffice, and (sector-specific) regulation of the (remaining) monopoly would only be a temporary phenomenon. Of course, it never turned out like this.

Two approaches to monopoly regulation

All economists agree that monopolies are inefficient when it comes to welfare, and thus regulatory intervention can be justified. But there are still two approaches when it comes to regulatory intervention, and which one is preferred very much depends on cultural approaches and sensitivities:

- The historically dominant approach pertains to competition regulation and is not particularly geared toward the network industries. It is also the American way to de- and re-regulate. Competition regulation comes after the fact – also called "ex-post-regulation" – and does not focus on the monopoly itself but on the abuse of the monopoly position by the monopolist. Such abuses can occur in any industry, and competition regulators are thus not sector-specific regulators. Competition regulation, which has a strong theoretical foundation, takes the form of regulating mergers and acquisitions, as well as the form of correcting (ex-post) the abuse of dominant positions. Competition regulation was used before sector-specific regulation emerged during the 1990s in Europe, mostly by US anti-trust authorities to break up infrastructure monopolies, most prominently in the case of the break-up of telecom monopolist AT&T in 1982 (Coll, 1988).
- The historically more novel approach, as promoted by the EC, aims at unbundling monopolies by unbundling competitive activities from activities that constitute so-called "natural monopolies." Natural monopolies, from a purely economic point of view, pertain to activities where the costs of creating competition are higher than the benefits that would be derived from such competition. Once identified, such natural monopolies will then be regulated in an ex-ante manner by sector-specific regulators, as natural monopolies are very different from sector to sector. The regulation of natural and other monopolies will be discussed in Chapter 5. This unbundling raises the question as to how to determine what constitutes a natural monopoly in the network industries, and thus what justifies sector-specific regulation and regulators.

How to determine natural monopolies?

As mentioned, a natural monopoly, from an economist's point of view, exists when the cost of creating competition exceeds its benefits. Of course, this very much depends on how one defines the relevant market. But in the network industries, market definition, as least in the beginning of liberalization, was not (yet) a problem, as markets were identical to the people served by the SOE. If liberalization caused competition with the SOE to occur naturally, then there was no such natural monopoly and therefore no need for sector-specific ex-ante regulation.

As a next step, one has to examine whether "sunk costs" are involved. Sunk costs have two economic effects: first they complicate market entry, as competitors have to risk large amounts of money to compete. Second and more importantly, sunk costs typically are at the origin of economies of scale, leading to the fact that the incumbent – once he has invested into its infrastructure – basically only incurs marginal costs, which again makes market entry of competitors difficult. If there are no such sunk costs, as is the case in the postal sector, for example, there is no natural monopoly, at least according to economic theory, and therefore no need for sector-specific ex-ante regulation. It did not turn out this way in practice, as we will see in Chapter 7.

Next, one must examine whether sunk costs are stable over time, as technological developments and innovations may well make these sunk costs obsolete; new entrants can easily enter these infrastructure markets thanks to new technologies. The typical example here is telecommunications, where mobile technology (it has been argued) allowed new market entrants to compete with incumbents. In theory, therefore, no sector-specific telecommunications regulation and regulator would be needed. But of course, the reality is different again, as we will see.

After these three "tests," one would be left with stable, natural monopolies or rather "monopolistic bottlenecks," where it would be justified to apply sector-specific ex-ante regulation. But even here, one may ask whether the cost of regulation does not exceed its benefits. Of course, this is a purely theoretical question, which is rarely asked, mainly because regulation is a dynamic process of gradual bureaucratization. I will discuss the institutional dynamics and corresponding costs of regulation in Chapter 4.

Applying such economic reasoning, one would conclude that only a limited number of network industry activities would constitute such monopolistic bottlenecks and justify sector-specific regulation and regulators. These activities are currently air traffic control (but not airlines and airports), railway infrastructures (tracks and signals but not trains and stations), the electricity and gas transmission and distribution grids (but not electricity generation and retail), and the drinking and wastewater pipes (but not retail). But this list is far too simplistic, even for some economists, and corresponds to only a small portion of today's regulatory reality. Consequently, network and regulatory economics have emerged to reflect and to theorize on the reality of network industry regulation after liberalization.

From network economics to regulatory economics

Network economics is a rapidly emerging new orientation of economics, especially in Europe. It mainly reflects the thinking of the few economists who have taken infrastructure systems seriously, starting often with tele-communications (Knieps, 2014) and then venturing out into electricity (Künneke, 2008). Its starting point is the technological reality of infrastructures, which are always complex and dynamic systems with nodes and links among them. Such systems clearly have fundamentally different economic characteristics than traditional atomistic markets, in which lots of producers compete against each other for customers who can choose freely.

I have already mentioned (direct) network effects as being the main driver for the monopolistic nature of the different network industries, a process further enhanced in the case of asset-specific industries with high sunk costs. But such direct or traditional network effects are still mainly about critical mass and economies of scale. Network economics goes further than such traditional network effects, inasmuch as it identifies additional economic implications of (technological) networked systems, namely compatibility, complementarity, tipping, and economics of system. Of course, each of these economic considerations will have implications for regulation.

From incompatibility to regulating interconnection

To understand the problem of the (in)compatibility of the technological networks, recall the history of the network industries, developed from the bottom-up; that is, from the local to the national to international levels. Rail networks, for example, have different gauges, different signaling systems, and different electricity systems. Electricity networks have different voltage levels, water networks have different pipe diameters, postal networks have different letter and parcel formats, and so on. Consequently, interconnection can be difficult because of technical incompatibilities.

Typically, the problem arises when markets are being opened by way of unbundling and operators from different countries want to access the infrastructure in another country. But historically, of course, this was also the case when local networks were integrated into national ones. Such technical incompatibilities can constitute impediments to competition, market integration, and ultimately demand and industry growth. Inversely, incompatibilities can be a way to foreclose a market and keep competitors out. In addition, the above-mentioned network effects cannot fully unfold, which can be interpreted as a market inefficiency due to a lack of standardization. This, in turn, justifies regulatory intervention, in particular technical interconnection regulation, so as to prevent technical barriers to competition, make networks more technically integrated, and ultimately increase efficiency and welfare.

From complementarity to regulating interoperability

The particular nature of the network industries pertains to the fact that services are provided on the basis of physical infrastructures such as roads, rail tracks, electricity and gas grids, and water pipes, as well as copper wires, fiber cables, and cell phone towers. Services and infrastructures are thus complementary. But the complementary nature is extreme, far beyond a "normal" relationship, such as between a printer and its cartridge. Such "strong complementarities" make it impossible for new services providers to use the infrastructure; for example, certain airplanes cannot communicate with air traffic control, and certain locomotives cannot use certain rail infrastructures.

Weak complementarities make usage possible, but the service provider negatively affects the infrastructure, such as badly maintained trucks and trains damaging the roads and tracks or particularly acidic water damaging pipes. Inversely, certain infrastructures negatively affect the service; for example, certain electricity grids or transformers negatively affect the quality of the electricity services (for example, with blackouts), badly maintained tracks damage trains, and leaking pipes lose water. All these negative effects negatively affect competition, market integration, and welfare.

On the other hand, a lack of compatibility or interoperability can help incumbents keep new entrants out, foreclose markets, and erect technical barriers to competition. In other words, to make markets more efficient and ultimately help deploy the full potential of network effects, interoperability has to be standardized, and standards in turn have to be regulated. Yet standards can also have negative economic effects, namely so-called lock-in and a lack of dynamic efficiencies.

From tipping to regulating congestion

All networks have physical limitations: there is only so much gas or water one can push through the pipes; there is only so much electricity that can be transported by the grid; there are only so many cars, trucks, trains, parcels, or airplanes that can be handled by a given infrastructure. Unlike in typical industries, production cannot scale linearly with demand. In the infrastructure, an additional unit of demand may tip over the system, in that such additional demand can only be handled by substantial additional investments. An economic consideration must be made between increasing infrastructure investment and by doing so increasing unit costs or curtailing demand and thus diminishing welfare. A congested infrastructure can still be economically more efficient but requires regulation to allocate the limited infrastructure in an economically efficient and especially non-discriminatory way. A congested infrastructure might also be a means to foreclose the market, keep competitors out, and ultimately take advantage of a monopoly position.

From economies of system to unbundling

Combining the above three network characteristics and corresponding economic effects, one can easily understand that a vertically integrated operator who controls interconnections, interoperability, bottlenecks, and tipping points can take advantage of what has been called "economies of system." Controlling the entire system allows the vertically integrated operator to take the most advantage of direct network effects; that is, being able to optimally match supply and demand. If one wants to increase the geographical scope of such network effects – for example, by passing from a national to a European system – one has to regulate interconnection, interoperability, and congestion, as the EC is trying to do.

Quite logically, unbundling appears to be the second-best solution, considering that one single EU-wide vertically integrated operator is a political no-go. Competition, it is argued, can only fully unfold its potential (for welfare) in fully unbundled infrastructure systems, as regulation of imperfectly unbundled systems will never be able to make them economically as efficient as full unbundling would. But, to be clear, even unbundling does not do away with the need to manage interconnection, interoperability, and congestion, which will have to be regulated regardless. As I will show later on, full unbundling actually complicates matters.

Public goods and their regulation

The economic theory that starts out by distinguishing between different types of goods (and services) leads to a totally different approach to regulation than what has been discussed so far. Unlike the European approach, which aims at perfecting markets, if need be by way of regulation, the US approach builds on the assumption that certain goods will never be offered by the free market.

The economic theory of goods builds on the distinction between public and private goods as the two extremes, with toll or club goods and common property goods as intermediaries. The underlying variables discriminating between public and private goods are excludability and rivalry. In the case of private goods, customers who do not pay can easily be excluded, and demand is directly correlated with scarcity or exhaustibility (the higher the demand, the scarcer the good) and thus directly affects the price. As for (pure) public goods, customers or citizens cannot be excluded (sometimes for social equity reasons), and demand does not directly affect scarcity or exhaustibility. Consequently, the pricing of public goods is difficult, and firms cannot make a profit with such goods. Street lighting is often mentioned as a typical public good.

As for common property goods, customers – or rather users – cannot (easily) be excluded, yet the good is scarce, leading rapidly to its exhaustion if its usage is not properly managed. "Commons" (for example, oceans, air, the climate) are considered to be typical common property goods. In this classification, infrastructures are considered to be typical toll goods or club goods: customers can easily be excluded (if they do not pay for infrastructure services), yet these goods are less scarce or exhaustible, owing to the very nature of infrastructures (for example, sunk costs, tipping).

Thus arises the question of the optimal or "right" price for such toll or club goods, as provided by the "utilities," to use the US terminology. Recall that in the US context, local utilities provide water, public transport, electricity, cable, gas, telecom, and other such services, at least in the past in a monopolistic fashion. Users – or rather citizens – can in theory be excluded but in practice must be served for political (social equity) reasons. Also, the cost of providing utility services does not increase linearly with demand, given the very nature of these infrastructures (sunk costs, tipping).

All this has led, historically, to the need for the regulation of such toll or club goods by local (state-level) public utility or public services commissions (see also Chapter 4). These commissions have to consider that utility service providers are profit-seeking entities but also that the price mechanism (supply and demand) does not operate as it should and that some users/citizens cannot be excluded from the services or rather that prices should be affordable. This, in turn, leads to a complicated science and practice of so-called "rate-making," which is another word for pricing the infrastructure services so that the providers can make a profit, yet the public interests are also considered.

Conclusion

The European and the US approaches to network industries could not be more different: if the European approach considers network industries to entail technical features that can potentially distort the market, the US approach considers that infrastructure goods are of a different nature (that is, they are toll or club goods) where the typical pricing mechanism does not apply. In the European approach, regulation tries to substitute for market conditions (yet reflecting as truthfully as possible market conditions); in the US approach, regulation is basically a form of arbitration between the public and the private interests. This US approach is actually fully in line with the American legal system, whereby courts ultimately arbitrate conflicting interests.

Both approaches have problems, as we will see later in this book. The European approach has great difficulty handling the public interest and public services in general. The US approach is not made for liberalization and competition; it has difficulty handling competing utility service providers, given that it was originally created to arbitrate rates between users/citizens and monopolistic (local) profit-seeking utilities.

3   The politics of regulation

Network industries have a political origin, as they were part and parcel of nation-building and continue to be foundational for any economy or society up to today. Their liberalization was based on political decisions, as evidenced by the World Bank and EU approaches. Economic theory was used to justify such liberalization, and regulatory economics are now used to design and politically justify their (re-)regulation. This is why sector-specific regulators are often also called "economic regulators." Still, both de- and re-regulation constitute politically decided intervention into the market, and this is precisely why we talk here about the politics of regulation.

That said, regulation – and the politics of regulation – is the result of the European approach rather than the American one. In the United States, "regulatory policies" are enacted at the state level by public utility regulatory commissions, and such "policies" ultimately end up, by way of litigation, being made by the courts. Also, regulators in the United States are much more political and sometimes even elected by the population.

In addition, some conceptual clarification must be made here, as the word "regulation" has a very different meaning in the US context than it does in the continental European context. In the US context, "regulation" basically denotes any kind of government intervention into the market and society, whereas in the continental European and especially the EU context, "regulation" is basically a technical or even technocratic term. It basically denotes the technicalities of creating and perfecting markets, something that can in large part be explained by the fact that regulation, in Europe, is promoted by the European Commission (EC), the technocratic arm of the EU. Nevertheless, as said above, regulation ultimately relies on political decisions. In the first section of this chapter, I present the political reality of regulation, as currently performed mainly in Europe by the different regulatory authorities. In the second section, I identify the main dimensions of regulatory intervention into the network industry, along with the main arguments used to justify such intervention.

The political reality of regulation

If one looks at what sector-specific regulators actually do, or rather have come to do over time, one finds a series of actions, grouped here into five dimensions, some based on economic, some on technical, and some on political arguments. The below typology is thus not derived from theory but rather from the observation of what regulators concretely do in their everyday practices.

Surveillance of market distortions (non-discrimination regulation)

Regulators are naturally worried about all kind of market distortions and try to prevent them as well as they can. And market distortions in the infrastructure are everywhere, owing to the history, the technological nature, the political interferences, and the policies affecting the different network industries. The most important distortions observed in many of the network industries follow.

- The pricing of the monopolistic infrastructure used by the different competing operators, one of which may be the owner of the infrastructure, may be distorted. It goes without saying that the price for using the infrastructure should be non-discriminatory; that is, the same for all operators. More often than in pricing, market discrimination results from inequitable access to the monopolistic infrastructure. Again, all operators using the infrastructure should have non-discriminatory access to it, and operations of the monopolistic infrastructure should not discriminate among operators. This potential discrimination and the discriminations listed below are especially a problem in the case of imperfect unbundling; that is, when the infrastructure manager is still a service provider.
- All infrastructures have physical limitations, or scarce capacity. Such scarce capacity should also be allocated in a non-discriminatory manner. Typically, auctioning of such scarce capacity – a market mechanism – is recommended to deal with this problem, but sometimes a system's integrity considerations prevent it (see below).
- Discrimination is also possible when it comes to the development of and investment in the infrastructures. Again, infrastructure development should be done in a way that does not discriminate against or favor one or several of the operators using the infrastructure. In addition, it should be done in a welfare-maximizing way; that is, in a way that such investments not only benefit all operators equally but moreover benefit the consumers and society in the long run – a truly challenging task for regulators.

Surveillance of the pricing of the infrastructure

Regulators should make sure that the price of the infrastructure is "correct," but what a correct price is can be subject to interpretation. There is substantial economics literature about the pricing of the monopolistic infrastructure, discussed in Chapter 5. But the reality of infrastructure pricing is actually different, as the regulator not only has to make sure that the price reflects an efficient infrastructure; he also has to balance such static efficiency with a dynamic one, where political considerations about "security of supply" or "sustainable infrastructure" come into play.

Surveillance of technical regulations

The surveillance of technical regulations is, according to pure theory, not part of sector-specific regulation and should in principle be done by other regulators, as is sometimes the case in electricity and is the case when it comes to nuclear safety. Still, regulators have, over time, come to be involved in technical regulations, given that technical features of infrastructures can lead to discriminations and in any case generate costs that can potentially be socialized. Such technical regulations typically pertain to connections to the infrastructure; regulators must decide whether or not these connections are part of the infrastructure (and as such if their costs can or cannot be socialized). Technical regulations also pertain to interoperability standards, which affect the integrity of the infrastructure or even the entire networked system. And many regulators are also active in safety matters, which again should be handled by safety agencies but are often handed over to sector-specific regulators.

Surveillance of public policy objectives

Many regulators do purely political regulation; that is, they regulate public policy objectives to be achieved by the operators, typically by the incumbents. The most common case is when politicians impose public or universal services obligations upon particular service providers, such as railway companies or postal services. Regulators are charged with monitoring whether these obligations are fulfilled. The justification for such political regulatory activity stems from the fact that subsidies and cross-subsidies are often involved, which in turn entails the possibility for market distortions. This topic will be further addressed in Chapter 5. But this surveillance of public policy objectives can go much further and encompass environmental objectives, labor conditions, or even contractual arrangements agreed upon with the government or even among operators. What regulators do in this respect is almost limitless and stems simultaneously from their own strategic behavior (to increase their remit and power), as well from the ever-expanding tasks governments impose upon them.

Surveillance of system integrity

This last activity of regulators is much fuzzier and is definitely beyond the typical attributions of an economic regulator. Rather it has to do with the foundational (and ultimately political) as well as the technological and systemic nature of infrastructure systems. Surveillance of an infrastructure system's integrity – called for example "system adequacy" in the case of electricity systems – results directly from liberalization, unbundling, and fragmentation of the system. Whereas traditionally vertically integrated SOEs took care of system integrity, this task must now be assumed by regulation and ultimately by regulators.

Arguments for regulation

From the above practices of regulation, one can identify three main functions that network industry regulation fulfills, namely creating and perfecting markets (economic regulation), protecting consumers (political regulation), and ensuring system integrity and continuity (technical regulation). I will present each function separately and discuss the argumentation it is grounded upon.

Creating and perfecting markets (economic regulation)

Markets in the network industries were non-existent before their liberalization and are far from perfect after. Since privatization was promoted by the World Bank as not being a credible approach to liberalization, unbundling has by now established itself as being most effective at creating infrastructure markets. However, creating and perfecting markets in more or less unbundled infrastructures requires often heavy-handed regulation.

• In many network industries, natural monopolies will remain even after liberalization; for example, in the case of railway tracks or electricity grids. These monopolies will have to be regulated, as users should not pay for an inefficient monopoly. The argument for such regulation is purely economic; different economic theories exist on how to regulate such natural monopolies, and the regulator, in this case, can be seen as a substitute for the market (see also Chapter 5).

- Competitors – including the more or less perfectly unbundled incumbent – must have access to this infrastructure. Again, such access must be regulated for non-discrimination, both in terms of access per se and pricing of the use of the infrastructure. The argument for why access has to be regulated is again economic, especially pertaining to network economics, as technical complementarities between infrastructure and operations (for example, standards) can lead to foreclosure. Full institutional unbundling, combined with market mechanisms to address potential congestions, are supposed to ultimately solve this problem.
- Competition issues may exist among the service providers using the monopolistic infrastructure, beyond unequal access conditions. Competition may be hampered by the market power of the incumbent, even if this incumbent is perfectly unbundled from the infrastructure manager, owing to direct network effects as well as to economies of scale. Again, the argumentation here is purely economic, and the regulator's role is to avoid resulting market distortions. However, the idea is that such regulation is temporary and will no longer be necessary once the new entrants have established themselves. In order to help new entrants, even asymmetric regulation may be authorized for a limited duration. In other words, the regulator not only has to make sure competition works, he even has to create the market; that is, create the conditions for the new entrants to exist.

Protecting consumers, or universal service regulation (political regulation)

According to neoliberal economic theory, a functioning market is the most efficient means to protect consumers, as markets optimize welfare. Such reasoning only applies to private goods, however. In the case of public, common property, or toll goods (as is the case in infrastructures), where markets are said to fail, rates must be regulated so as to accommodate both the consumers and the firms. But such reasoning works for monopolies only and is grounded in the idea that markets either fail (toll goods, in the case of infrastructures) or do not fail (private goods).

With liberalization, this black and white distinction no longer holds: competing service providers can choose to serve selected customers, and some customer-citizens may simply not be served any longer in liberalized markets, unless some firms are subsidized by the government to provide the service as a public service. In other words, some consumer-citizens have to be protected not because the market fails but because it succeeds.

At the time when there were still public monopolies, cross-subsidies made it possible to serve even the non-paying consumer-citizens. This practice was called, in the Latin (but not the Anglo-Saxon) tradition, "public service." The public monopoly (SOE) provided a public service or was even called a "public service company." With liberalization, this practice is no longer possible as the SOE, which may have become partially or totally privatized in the meantime, has to compete against new entrants and can no longer afford to do so. Some customer-citizens may no longer be served once competition takes hold.

The use of subsidies or cross-subsidies is, in my opinion, the only logical reasoning adopted by the EC, and it has become an integral part of network industry regulation since the beginning of deregulation in the EU; that is, an integral part of the European regulatory approach. Ever since the beginning of deregulation, regulation and regulators have had to protect these consumer-citizens that used to be served by the traditional public monopoly (SOE) but were no longer served in a liberalized market. The intellectual trick of the EC was to redefine the vaguely defined and rarely enforced public services that used to be provided by the SOEs in terms of legally enforceable consumer protection and precisely defined consumer rights. This became called a universal service or universal service obligation (USO), which was then imposed upon one of the market players, typically the incumbent, as the new entrants were rarely interested in the USO.

However, when it came to the definition of the USO, the EC referred back to the traditional French legal definition of public service, namely the service that a government provides to its citizens through an SOE: equity, continuity, and affordability.

- Equity meant that all citizens should be treated equally. When translated into the USO, this came to mean that the same categories of consumers should be treated equally. For example, the price of the stamp is the same no matter where the consumers live and send their mail to (on the national territory). However, prices for firms may be different.
- Continuity of service originally meant that the public monopoly had to provide the service over time to its citizens, ideally indefinitely. In its EU version, continuity now means that consumers have a right to a list of legally defined services. At times, the term "accessibility to services" is also used here.
- Affordability meant that the public service provided by the historical public monopoly must be affordable to its citizens. In the EU universal service terminology, affordability now means that consumers have the right to affordable services as politically defined.

Given that neither the incumbent nor the new entrant has a commercial interest to provide such universal services, the USO will be legally imposed upon one of the operators, typically the incumbent. The role of the regulator then is to make sure that this operator delivers but also that the provider of these services does not derive undue, market-distorting advantages from this obligation.

System integration and system continuity (technical regulation)

System integrity and system continuity are much more recent regulatory functions that have appeared in some of the most technologically dominated network industries, namely in electricity, gas, railways, air transport, and water. It is not obvious how to regulate system integrity and system continuity; the regulators seem to gradually take charge or are put in charge by politicians.

The argument for regulating system integrity is primarily a technological one: infrastructures are complex and dynamic systems that function optimally as systems. Over time, standards have developed that make these systems ever more complex and ever more integrated. Unbundling these systems was originally a political decision. Unbundling became necessary when the EU wanted to create an internal market, beyond the traditional national boundaries of these systems. As a result of unbundling, many interfaces – especially the interfaces between the monopolistic infrastructure and the services as provided by several operators – became more difficult to manage, leading in turn to higher costs. We have already seen how network effects and economies of systems naturally push toward monopolization (or, in more technical language, system integration); vertically integrated technological systems are typically more efficient (if properly regulated), but they are also monopolies. A single, monopolistic, vertically integrated, EU-wide infrastructure system, the logical outcome of such reasoning, would simply not be acceptable for political reasons.

Before liberalization, the system integrator used to be the SOE. Coordination across national borders was done among the SOEs of the different countries themselves, usually without political intervention or oversight. But in a liberalized, unbundled, fragmented, and increasingly competitive environment, the responsibility for system integration reverts back to the ones who liberalized and unbundled the system; that is, the public authorities. They delegate this responsibility to the regulator. Indeed, the regulator is the only actor to have a neutral or non-interested overview of the different parts of the system and how they relate to each other. As technological infrastructures become ever more complex and more intensely used, the pressure to make the regulator into a system integrator will only increase. The drawback is that the regulator can only regulate or make rules; he cannot operate the system in real time, which makes him less efficient as a system integrator (because of "regulatory costs") than the original monopolist was.

System continuity is another matter, even though system continuity requires, at least to a certain extent, system integration. The argument for system continuity is not a technical one but is primarily a political one and as such stems from the public services idea, in particular the idea that infrastructure services must have continuity. System continuity is grounded in the idea that infrastructures constitute a foundational economy that is essential for the functioning of the national economy and society. Yet one can add some economic reasoning: while liberalization leads to more static efficiencies, it may put at risk long-term investment into maintaining, improving, and developing infrastructure into the future. Operators will have little incentive to invest in uncertain future assets, thus jeopardizing the continuity of service. Yet public authorities cannot afford to put system continuity at risk, and typically monitor or even mandate investment.

In this chapter, I have argued that regulation is a primarily political activity that relies on economic, technological, and political arguments, arguments that become increasingly blurred. This blurring is somewhat paradoxical, as network industry regulators are considered to be economic regulators only. Also, the activities of regulators have significantly evolved over time – and will continue to do so – because liberalization has generated issues and problems (such as public services and system continuity) that are addressed by more regulation. In addition, as we will see later in this book, the traditional technologies in the different infrastructures have also evolved, in part because of liberalization, creating new issues and calling again for more regulation.

Such sector-specific regulation and regulatory policies have been accompanied by the creation of sector-specific regulatory authorities, whose task it is to put into practice these at-times-contradictory regulatory policies. These authorities also constitute a new and unprecedented organizational and institutional reality, which has the potential to develop a dynamic of its own. This will be the topic of the next chapter.

4 Regulatory authorities

This chapter addresses another, equally important dimension of the politics of regulation, namely the creation of regulatory authorities. We have already seen that the liberalized network industries would not function without regulation. Similarly, regulation would not exist without regulators. Regulators are at least as important as regulation itself because regulators have much discretionary power. They are the ones who put regulation into practice. Also, regulators EU-style are not just a novelty for the liberalized network industries; they are also a novelty for the traditional politico-administrative system. As such, regulators, regulatory authorities, or regulatory bodies, as they are often called, clearly deserve an entire chapter.

This chapter is structured as follows: in the first section, I recall the institutional aspects of the US model of regulation. The second section goes into more depth in regard to the EU-type, sector-specific, independent regulator, as this type of regulator seems to be rapidly becoming the model worldwide. The third section specifically discusses the competencies and powers of this sector-specific regulator, as even the best institutional structure and regulatory body remains toothless without power. The last section is devoted to the institutional dynamics resulting from the creation of EU-style, sector-specific regulators and highlights some of the problems that may result from their creation in the future, such as the costs of regulation and potential political backlash.

The institutional aspects of the US model[1]

Regulators do not fit into the politico-administrative landscape, at least in Europe. Indeed, in the European member states, the emergence of independent regulatory authorities is an institutional novelty and as such basically the result of EU regulatory policy during the 1990s. The story is somewhat different in the United States, where regulators have a much longer history, which in turn can be explained by the federalist nature of the United States. In the United States, regulators – the so-called public utilities regulatory commissions or public services regulatory commissions – go back to the period of rapid development of the infrastructures at the turn of the 20th century. Given the relative independence of the 50 US states, each of the states built up its respective utilities' regulators, which led to some diversity. Utilities regulators cover all utilities, namely electricity, gas, public transport, water, and even cable TV and others.

I have already shown in Chapter 2 that the underlying theory of such utilities' regulation was the theory of public goods: utilities were considered to be delivering toll or club goods and, as such, were regulated as monopolies. In other words, the utility enjoys an exclusive franchise over a given territory, typically the entire state or a city. As part of that franchise, utilities are protected from competition and antitrust law. The utility also enjoys the right of eminent domain, the recovery of approved costs, a reasonable opportunity to earn a fair return, and the right to charge for the cost of service. In exchange, the utility "has the obligation to provide all paying customers with access to safe, adequate, reliable, convenient and non-discriminatory service on just and reasonable terms, while assuming certain business and market risks and subjecting itself to regulatory reporting, reviews and oversight" (Beecher).

In other words, the utilities commit to some sort of "regulatory compact." The main dimensions of this regulatory compact are the commitment to a universal service, a given service portfolio, service efficiency, operational standards, service reliability, and quality, as well as capacity utilization. This compact further includes much broader commitments to consumer education, public and worker safety, and economic development. The regulator, in turn, makes sure that the compact is adhered to. This relative lack of precision is counter-balanced by the US legal system. Indeed, regulators and utilities typically end up before courts, first at the state and ultimately at the federal level.

Over the past 80 years, some jurisprudence has been established by the US Supreme Court. Beecher has summarized the key jurisprudence as follows:

- Returns are authorized but not guaranteed.
- Regulation involves the "fair interpretation of a bargain."
- Returns should reflect "corresponding risk."
- Regulators should not substitute their judgment for "board discretion."
- Prudence is presumed, but "wasteful" expenditures should be disallowed.
- Rate base property must be "used and useful" to ratepayers.
- Regulation does not ensure that businesses will produce "net revenues."

- Regulators are not bound by formulas and are free to make "pragmatic" adjustments.
- Due process does not insure or protect utilities from losses due to "economic forces."
- A contract rate is not "'unjust' or 'unreasonable' simply because it is unprofitable."
- Utilities must "operate with all reasonable economies."
- Regulators should not usurp management or judge prudence based on "20/20" hindsight.
- Courts allow regulators to decide within a "zone of reasonableness."
- Rate methodologies should not arbitrarily shift risks to and from investors.

Looking at this jurisprudence, one can see that regulators have substantial freedom of interpretation, and the same is true for the regulated utilities. The ultimate "regulator," however, is the courts and, in the end, the Supreme Court. This is the US model of regulation.

So, who are these regulators or public utilities regulatory commissions? First, they are as diverse as the 50 US states. Each state has its own regulatory commission, with little standardization, and especially no federal rules, as to the structure and powers of these regulators. Typically, these regulators are structured into a set of commissioners who ultimately make the decisions and a staff who does the work. The commissioners are either appointed by the governor of the state or directly elected by the population of the state. Commissioners therefore have a political color. Yet their political inclinations are again checked by the courts. In this way and over time, some regulatory stability nevertheless emerges.

Yet another dimension of the US regulatory system is the federal regulators. Indeed, state utility regulators do have limitations: over time, utilities – especially electricity, gas, and telecommunications – have come to cover several states and even the entire US territory. Electricity and gas, for example, may be produced in one state and sold in another. Telecommunications operators, after the breakup of AT&T, started to compete. The state level is no longer the only level, and perhaps no longer the most appropriate level, at which utilities need to be regulated. Consequently, over time some national regulators have emerged, such as the FCC – the Federal Communications Commission – and FERC – the Federal Energy Regulatory Commission. Yet the United States remains a federalist system, that is, a subsidiary and bottom-up system, and these federal regulatory commissions are only competent when it comes to interstate matters. It is thus fair to say that the US regulatory system needs to be reformed. And this is where the much more recent EU model comes in.

The EU model of an independent, sector-specific regulator

When it comes to its institutional dimensions, the European model could not be more different from the US model:

- If the US model is a bottom-up and a subsidiary model, the EU model is just the opposite. In the United States, the utilities' regulators make decisions at the state level. These decisions, over time and thanks to jurisprudence, achieve some sort of federal legitimacy. Federal regulators can only act where interstate matters are concerned. In contradistinction, the European model is a top-down model, where all the rules are decided at the supra-national level, including the way national regulators should be structured and operate.
- If the US utilities' regulators are mainly concerned with local monopolies and regulate these as toll or club goods, the EU model is concerned with Europe-wide competition, with the public goods or public service dimension being treated totally separately, as shown in Chapter 3.
- If the US model is quite political, the European model is basically technocratic. Indeed, since the US model deals with public goods and since regulators are politically appointed or even elected, US regulators are in fact political actors. In the EU, instead, regulation is seen as a technocratic matter, with regulators focusing mostly on the technicalities of imperfect competition. Consequently, the independence of the regulators from politics is much more important.
- Finally, if the US utilities' regulators are cross-sectoral, the EU regulatory model is sector-specific. Indeed, in the EU, there are no "utilities" regulators; instead there are energy regulators, telecommunication regulators, rail regulators, air transport regulators, postal regulators, and others.

Sector-specificity of regulators

The sector-specificity of the EU-type regulators is best understood if one compares them not with the cross-sectoral US utilities regulators but with the cross-sectoral competition regulators. Indeed, EU-type sector-specific regulators are much closer to competition regulators than are US-type utilities regulators, which explains the recently emerging problem of the EU regulators' overlap. Also, competition regulators have a long history in both continental Europe and the US world, as they were also created in the inter-war period or after the second World War in most industrializing countries and as such were inspired by US antitrust legislation. Basically, the idea of competition regulation is to prevent the abuse of dominant positions by incumbents, either because of dumping or predatory pricing. Also, competition regulators are cross-sectoral. Finally, competition regulation and regulators always come after the fact (ex-post regulation).

Competition regulation could have been applied in the European network industries, as it was in the United States when breaking up AT&T, the private telecom monopoly. Also, in some rare European countries, the initial steps toward liberalization relied on competition regulation and were done by competition regulators. But liberalization solely through competition regulation proved to be ineffective because of its incoherent nature as well as because of the numerous legal battles it generated. Using only competition regulation was also not the idea of the European Commission, as its goal was not just to break up national monopolies but, much more ambitiously, to create a real internal market. For that goal, ex-post regulation was far too weak and too unsystematic.

A sector-by-sector ex-ante approach appeared to be much more promising. As a matter of fact, each of the network industries had a national monopoly, and the market dominance of the monopolies was not simply due – as is assumed in competition regulation – to market power but to the industries' technological nature. And technology is different in each of the sectors. Technical impediments to competition were mainly seen as being located at the interfaces between the infrastructure and the services provided on the basis of the infrastructure. Consequently, the European Commission concluded that liberalization could only come from unbundling; that is, from the vertical separation of the monopolistic infrastructure (the grid, the track, the tubes, the cables) and the services provided on the basis of this monopolistic infrastructure (the train service, the electricity service, the water service, the telecommunications service). In regulatory terms, this approach raises the question of access to the monopolistic infrastructure by competitors, something that competition regulation cannot really handle, as this requires the ex-ante definition of access conditions and access pricing, including the regulation of technical standards.

Because unbundling was – and still is – not perfect, the sector-specific regulator also needs to understand operations, especially how infrastructures and services interact and influence each other, and how an imperfectly unbundled incumbent can take advantage of this interaction to discriminate against new entrants. And because, as we saw in Chapter 2, all these network industries are complex technical systems, the regulator also needs a sound and comprehensive understanding of how these systems work as systems.

Independence of regulators

The preoccupation with the independence of the sector-specific regulators is not European. We find the same preoccupation in the US when it comes to utilities' regulators. It is, of course, also a preoccupation for competition regulators. Indeed, a significant portion of the literature about regulators has been devoted to so-called "regulatory capture," although this concept only focuses on the question of the independence of the regulators from the regulated firms. And this is indeed a problem, especially in the network industries, which require technical expertise. Generally, such expertise can only be acquired while working in the industry itself. Competent sector-specific regulators, especially commissioners, have previously worked in the industry, where they have acquired their competence and knowledge.

All kind of provisions are therefore needed to make sure that these commissioners act independently of the firms they worked for earlier, as well as independently of the firms that would like to hire them once they are done being regulators. Such provisions may include attractive salaries for regulators so as not to be tempted by industry (the UK model), as well as contractual provisions, such as cooling-off periods. Since regulators do have significant powers over the industry in general and the regulated firms in particular, it is only logical that firms and industry organizations are trying to lobby regulators by all means available. There is nothing wrong with this lobbying, and industry lobbying may even be positive if it helps regulators to better understand how the industry works. Still, the very basis of the regulatory model lies in the independence of the regulators from the regulated firms.

A second element of regulatory independence is the independence of the regulators from politics. In the European model, independence from politics carries much more weight than is the case in the United States. Of course, at an abstract level, regulatory independence from day-to-day politics is equally important in Europe and the United States. But in the United States, the utility regulator has a much more political role. Rates, for example, should strike a balance between the firms' investment and operational needs, consumer protection, and the broader public interest. In the case of the European approach, however, regulators are first of all technocrats whose role it is to apply to the letter the rules set by politicians, more precisely the European Commission, and approved by Parliament and Council. Their leeway is thus quite limited. Courts of course also play a role but are much less important than in the United States; they basically decide whether regulators have respected the law set by the European Commission. And regulators' independence from politics, especially national or member state politics, is the guarantee of their stability and their predictability. In addition, such independence from politics is even more necessary since in Europe almost all infrastructure operators and still many services providers remain state-owned. Imperfect unbundling worsens the case. The independence of the regulators from politics is thus a matter of the credibility of the entire European regulatory approach.

This construct of an independent, sector-specific regulator is truly revolutionary. As such, independent, sector-specific regulators are probably the only significant institutional innovation since the emergence of the modern nation-state. They are neither policy makers, nor part of the administration in terms of policy advice, nor part of the judiciary. They are a new institutional construct that does not really fit into the politico-administrative landscape. As such, they may not be a stable construct. But more about that later.

The crucial issue: powers of the regulator

Regulators can be as independent as they want, but if they have no power, they remain toothless and ultimately ineffective. Regulatory power has many dimensions, such as legal mandate, resources, financing mechanism, selection process, track record, and, most importantly, power based on competence or expertise. At least in the European context, the power of the regulator derives from a clear legal basis: the law defines the remit of the regulator, namely in which matters the regulator can be active and in which not. Without such a clear legal basis, the regulator can simply not act. If he acts nevertheless, courts will disavow him. The law also defines the investigative and the sanctioning powers of the regulator. The legal mandate is important, but without investigative powers, regulators can often not substantiate their decisions. Also, if the regulator has sanctioning powers, such as imposing fines, regulated firms are generally more willing to cooperate.

A second important element that determines the power of the regulator is the regulator's resources. Resources can be financial, and money will mostly be used to hire staff or pay for supportive studies. But resources also pertain to competence and expertise. In short, regulators may look good on paper, with a substantial remit and even investigative and sanctioning powers, yet lack the resources and expertise to put these powers into regulatory action.

Money is not important only in absolute terms. The power of the regulator also depends on where the money comes from. Typically, regulators are financed by the government's budget, which in turn may make them somewhat dependent upon political decision. But parts of a regulator's financial resources can also stem from the fees the regulator charges for his decisions. They can even stem from the fines the regulator may inflict upon a firm. Yet levies and fines, while offering regulators some independence from government and politics, have the potential to create wrong incentives.

Selection and especially reappointment rules also determine, at least to a certain degree, the power of a regulator. There is quite a debate as to whether regulators should be allowed to be reappointed, as reappointment makes them somewhat more lenient vis-à-vis firms and politicians. Finally, as with corporate boards, regulators should be replaced in a staggered manner; otherwise, too much expertise might be lost at one time.

While all these factors are important to determine the power of a regulator, the most crucial factor, in my opinion, is the competence and expertise of the regulator. Indeed, all the above considerations cannot make up for a lack of competent staff and commissioners. And competence and expertise are needed by regulators not only to make decisions that pass in court but also to be appreciated by the regulated firms, as they will respect competent regulators.

Regulatory dynamics and related problems

I have argued that the independent, sector-specific regulator is an odd institutional construct within the traditional politico-administrative system. This section highlights the main implications the corresponding institutional dynamics lead to or may lead to in the future.

From national to EU regulators

Already today one can observe, in the case of Europe, a clear evolution toward EU regulators. The process is the same in all network industries. In a first step, a European directive mandates that member states set up sector-specific regulators. The remit and the powers of these regulators are very precisely defined in this and subsequent directives. However, quite rapidly, significant differences emerge among these national regulators: some grow rapidly and become very powerful, whereas others come to hardly exist. In a second step, therefore, the European Commission encourages these regulators to self-organize so as to harmonize their practices, the more advanced ones being encouraged to teach the less advanced ones. As a result, regulators' associations are formed; to my knowledge, this has occurred in all the sectors.

But then the European Commission becomes frustrated with these associations, which are generally too slow and do not really have the powers to bring the laggards along. Thus, in a third step, the European Commission creates its own sector-specific European regulator, in spite of and in addition to the regulators' associations. Again, this has happened in all the sectors, except in the postal sector. As this is an important step where power is removed from national regulators and given to European regulators, the European Commission proceeds with caution, first transferring powers to the European regulators in the least controversial areas, such as safety and other technical issues. But gradually, and this is the fourth step, even some economic regulatory powers are transferred to these European regulators.

At the very end of this process, the national regulators will be merely the executing agents of the European regulators, who are the executing agents of the European Commission. Note that no equivalent evolution has occurred in the United States, where the few federal regulators that exist are not a substitute of the state regulators but rather a competitor.

Who regulates the regulators?

In parallel with these European dynamics, institutional dynamics exist at the national level. Regulators take on more and more activities and extend their powers to a series of areas that are beyond their remit. Typically, the problem is that no one regulates the regulators. This evolution will ultimately engender political backlash and endanger the very existence of these sector-specific national regulators.

Regulators are, by their very nature, not regulated, as they are supposed to be independent both from politics and from the firms they regulate. To a certain extent, they are "regulated" by the courts, inasmuch as courts can invalidate decisions made by the regulators. If this happens too often, regulators lose credibility and gain a bad reputation, and reputation is indeed the only real resource they have in the long run. But courts only "regulate" regulators in regard to the decisions they make. Yet regulators do many other things for which the only limits are the financial resources (that is, the budget) and/or political oversight. Indeed, over time, regulators gradually venture into many activities. Often, there is no precise legal mandate that prevents them from doing so.

For example, from setting conditions for market entry of new operators, regulators can gradually move to granting market entry authorizations. Similarly, from approving tariffs, they may move to proposing and even to setting tariffs. From monitoring certain practices of the regulated operators – for example, accounting practices – they gradually move to monitoring operators altogether. Finally, from monitoring markets, they gradually are defining the conditions under which markets operate. In other words, if unchecked, regulators move beyond their original remit. Instead of correcting market failures, they will be setting the very conditions for the "market" as they think it should work. As the literature has mainly been concerned with regulatory capture by regulated firms, this phenomenon remains under-researched, yet seems equally problematic, at least in the European context.

Regulators as policy makers?

But there is more: there is a clear temptation for regulators to move into mediation and even into conflict resolution. This temptation comes from the fact that preparing regulatory decisions is time consuming and costly. By convening the parties and seeking an agreement among them or even with the regulator, precious time can be saved; this is something that firms often ask for themselves. However, once the regulator has been engaged in a mediation or conflict resolution process, he may have a problem issuing decisions, as he may no longer be impartial. A cultural dimension to conflict resolution also exists; regulation is, like the judiciary, based on a conflictual approach. Yet many regulators and many political cultures prefer a more consensual approach. It is my firm opinion that regulators should not be tempted by this easy road of mediation and conflict resolution.

Regulators, at least in the European approach, should strictly adhere to the law and make their decisions accordingly. If they do not, they will be sanctioned by the courts if attacked. However, the network industries are evolving rapidly, and regulators often have to decide on issues for which the legal basis is confusing, contradictory, or even absent. In such cases, they interpret the law or make up rules. If unchallenged, or if challenged yet approved by the courts, this behavior amounts to rule making by regulators. To a certain extent, this rule making is inevitable, given the dynamic nature of the network industries. Nevertheless, over time these small rule-making activities by regulators can amount to policy making, something which is clearly not a task of a regulator.

Even without making policy, regulators can gradually slide into the role of giving policy advice. This role especially occurs when regulators are highly competent; that is, when they have become more competent than the public administration, at least in certain technical matters. First the press but later parliament and even government will turn to regulators for advice. Giving policy advice is clearly another example of regulators overstepping their role over time. This may become problematic in the long run: regulators, at least in the European approach, are not democratically legitimated. Yet they may become political actors over time, which will trigger a political reaction or a political backlash, something like a "return of politics into regulation."

Sector-specific regulators as competition regulators?

A final interesting dimension of regulators' institutional dynamics pertains to competition regulation. As stated above, the relationship between sector-specific regulation and competition regulation has been problematic since the very beginning of sector-specific regulation and regulators. In theory, the relationship is clear: the sector-specific regulator is, among others, in charge of the monopoly. In the European approach, this is the price the monopolist can charge for the usage of his monopolistic infrastructure by the service providers. In the US approach, it is the rates the monopolist may charge to the consumers.

In addition, in the European approach, the sector-specific regulator is in charge of the broad relationships between the service providers (incumbent and new entrants) and the monopolistic infrastructure. In principle, the relationships among the service providers (incumbent and new entrants) are a matter of competition regulation. In reality, however, competition regulators have shied away from their responsibility in this area and left the field wide open to the sector-specific regulators, who then have become competition regulators. I consider this a very dangerous evolution: at some point, more regulations will make markets even less perfect, which in turn will require ever more regulation to remedy these imperfections – a truly vicious circle.

Regulatory costs

Institutional economics teaches us that institutions (that is rules) have a cost. Sector-specific and other regulations are a typical illustration of such costly institutions. Originally, institutional economists were only concerned with the cost of corporate governance; that is, with the information asymmetries resulting from the separation of ownership and control over firms. The application of institutional economics to the regulation and governance of the network industries came much later and led to relevant considerations about the cost of regulation versus its benefits (Ménard, 2000). And there are indeed many such costs to be considered, namely direct costs (such as the cost of the regulatory body), indirect costs (such as the costs a firm incurs when having to comply and even to lobby regulators), and induced costs, which pertain to the amount of money that is no longer available for innovation and firm development.

All the above considerations may well lead to the question of whether this European, independent, sector-specific regulator is indeed a stable model and especially a model that is able to survive national political backlash. And this question exists despite the fact that this European approach is, in my opinion, intellectually sound and superior to the US approach.

Note

1 I am thankful to Prof. Janice Beecher, Director, Institute of Public Utilities Policy Research & Education (IPU), Michigan State University, for her profound insights into US-style utility regulation and regulators.

5   Regulating monopolies

In this chapter, I discuss the regulation of natural monopolies as promoted by the European approach. We have already seen, in Chapters 2 and 4, how the United States regulates monopolies at the state level as toll or club goods through public utilities or public services regulatory commissions. In the next chapter, I will discuss yet another approach – a so-called "French model" – to "regulating" monopolies, namely by way of contracts, which in turn are being tendered.

The European approach discussed in this chapter applies to the remaining monopolistic part of unbundled utilities or public enterprises, namely infrastructures such as rail tracks, electricity grids (high and low voltage), gas pipelines, roads, air traffic control, and copper and fiber cables, as well as water and wastewater tubes. These infrastructures are so-called "natural monopolies"; that is, monopolistic infrastructure operators based on heavy assets, where the cost of creating competition would be higher than the benefits resulting from such competition. Services providers – such as train operating companies (TOCs), electricity and gas retailers, bus and taxi companies, airlines, shippers, telecom operators, and water services companies – need access to these monopolistic infrastructures to deliver their services. Therefore, not only access to but also the price for using these monopolistic infrastructures must be regulated. In this chapter, I discuss the three currently dominant ways of regulating this price: cost-plus (cost+) regulation, price-cap regulation, and various kinds of incentive regulation.

Cost+ or rate-of-return (RoR) regulation

Cost+ regulation, also called rate-of-return (RoR) regulation, is the most widespread form of regulating natural monopolies, at least in continental Europe. It is also the fairest; that is, the least arbitrary way of defining the price the service provider has to pay to use a monopolistic infrastructure, or the price the owner of the monopolistic infrastructure receives. It is also the most time-consuming and labor-intensive way of regulating monopolies.

Basically, cost+ regulation seeks to determine, as accurately as possible, the cost of operating and maintaining the infrastructure. To this cost, a profit margin is typically added – the "+" – to allow the monopolist to make a reasonable profit, sufficient to maintain existing infrastructure and replace obsolescent infrastructure. The goal of cost+ regulation is for the cost determined by regulators to be as close as possible to the exact costs of operating and maintaining the infrastructure. Renewal and development of the infrastructure is typically included, but sometimes major infrastructure developments are not part of the cost base. If this is the case, these infrastructure developments will be decided upon and financed by government or parliament.

Two major types of cost are typically considered when calculating the cost or asset base: operating costs (OPEX) and capital investments (CAPEX). Operating costs include all the costs incurred by the infrastructure owner to safely yet efficiently operate the infrastructure, such as labor costs and the costs of the energy to operate the infrastructure. To these costs, a profit margin, generally determined by the regulator, is added. This profit margin should be designed to allow the infrastructure owner or operator to generate a positive cashflow so as to be able to maintain, renew, and expand the infrastructure.

Operators borrow money to develop their infrastructures. These loans must be repaid and the corresponding investments discounted over quite a long period of time, considering that most infrastructures are long-lived assets. Typical repayment periods are 40 years or more. The infrastructure owner pays interest on the borrowed money. Yet firms generally borrow from a wide variety of sources with different interest rates. Therefore, regulators calculate an average interest rate, called WACC – the weighted average cost of capital. This WACC is what regulators usually apply when calculating the average interest rate that applies to all the loans taken by the infrastructure owner. In most cases, the WACC is determined by the regulator, but in some countries the WACC is determined by the political authorities, making it much more subject to lobbying: while the regulator would seek a WACC that most closely mirrors market rates, the political authorities are typically more generous when calculating the WACC.

The operating costs, the margins on the operating costs, the (annual) repayment of the investments, and the WACC constitute the RAB or regulatory asset base. Sometimes, additional elements will be added to this RAB, such as various taxes from local to national, sometimes including VAT and others. The regulator approves this RAB, which is then socialized – meaning that the users of the infrastructure will pay for the RAB, roughly pro rata to their usage. The RAB also determines how much the infrastructure owner earns.

Pros

There is much to be said for cost+ regulation, as it is quite fair, inasmuch as the regulator, if he puts sufficient means into it, can quite precisely define the costs of the monopolistic infrastructure. He can also detect all kinds of operating and investment inefficiencies and correct them, mainly by not including these inefficiencies into the RAB. He can even tailor the investments by approving some of them and excluding others.

Cons

But there are also cons: cost+ regulation is a quite intrusive way of regulating the monopolist. It is also time-consuming and costly. Problems can arise for the regulator not only in terms of lacking information but when it comes, for example, to distinguishing precisely between operating and investment costs.

The main con highlighted and criticized by the literature is the incentives given to the infrastructure monopolist by cost+ regulation: indeed, the infrastructure owner and manager has a clear incentive to inflate investments, something called "gold plating." The bigger the investments, namely the investments recognized by the regulator as being included in the RAB, the bigger the "profits" thanks to the WACC, the induced operating costs, and the related margins. Another incentive is to substitute labor with capital, as labor is typically more flexible, whereas investments into physical infrastructures, once approved by the regulator, will generate long-lasting returns. In short, cost+ regulation does not set incentives for the infrastructure operator to become more efficient, unless the regulator really forces him to. But if the regulator has the resources and is competent, he can easily do that. Otherwise, a better answer might well be some sort of incentive regulation.

Price-cap regulation

Price-cap regulation is an early form of incentive regulation, practiced mostly in the United Kingdom. Price-cap regulation sets a cap on the annual increase of the price the infrastructure may charge to the service provider, typically for a three- to five-year period. This is done in a relatively simple way, namely by setting an initial price – or simply by taking the current price – and then by defining a path by which this initial price is reduced. The regulator typically takes the retail price index (RPI) or some other consumer price index (CPI) and then subtracts from it a "productivity factor" x (RPI-x). This productivity factor is assumed to reflect the productivity increase that the firm can reasonably achieve during the time period. In this way, the infrastructure owner knows in advance what its income will be for the given period. It is incentivized to reduce its operational costs by an amount that is bigger than RPI-x since it can keep the cost savings made during the allotted time period (three to five years) as profits. After the three- to five-year period, the formula is typically recalculated to bring it in line with the underlying costs.

Cost+ regulation was initially aimed at regulating stable, long-lasting monopolistic infrastructures. Price-cap regulation was considered to be an intermediary step toward fully deregulated markets. In other words, price-cap regulation is considered to help regulated firms to prepare themselves for full deregulation.

Pros

Price-cap regulation has many advantages as compared to cost+ regulation: most importantly, price-cap regulation is easy and cheap to administer. In its simplest form, the regulator can start with existing retail prices and define a path to reduce them. Price-cap regulation also has the advantage of setting an incentive to become more efficient since all efficiency gains beyond RPI-x can be kept by the regulated firm. Furthermore, it incentivizes regulated firms to become more innovative, as new services generally do not fall under price-cap regulation.

Cons

The first and probably the main problem of price-cap regulation is its arbitrariness: are the prices right from the start? And if not, from which price should one start? Since price-cap regulation is not as intrusive as cost+ regulation, the regulator does not need to fully understand the accounting of the regulated firm and therefore is not really capable of judging whether the retail prices practiced by the regulated firm make any sense. However, taking the existing retail prices as a starting point can make perfect sense in the perspective of incentivizing the regulated firms to become more market oriented and dynamic.

Choosing the index is also somewhat arbitrary: will the regulator use the RPI or the CPI? Will he use a general index that covers most industries, or will he seek out an industry-specific RPI? Will he use a national or a more international index? But then, by definition, infrastructure is not really a competitive industry, and corresponding indexes are hard to come by. There is also arbitrariness in defining RPI-x. Will it be an overall productivity index across all the industries? Or are there industry-specific productivity indexes? In short, how will the regulator arrive at a "correct" x; that is, at a "correct" incentive?

In addition, if price-cap regulation is used repeatedly – beyond a second or even a third regulatory period – it loses its incentivizing power. The initial retail prices are adjusted to the new and lower ones, and even the productivity factor may be adjusted and lowered if the regulated firm makes "too high" profits. These adjustments incentivize the regulated firm to lower its efficiency gains, as they may be regulated away anyway. In other words, if price-cap regulation lasts too long, it may end up looking like cost+ regulation.

Finally, if cost+ regulation incentivizes over-investments or gold-plating, price-cap regulation does the opposite, incentivizing under-investments. Indeed, the price-cap regulated firm may well save on its investments so as to generate short-term profits, which it can keep. The literature has therefore highlighted some serious problems of price-cap regulation, as it encourages managerial short-termism and even short-sightedness.

Incentive regulation

If price-cap regulation is an early form of incentive regulation, much more advanced or sophisticated forms exist. One can distinguish between two further types of incentive regulation, namely performance regulation and benchmarking regulation. Both types of incentive regulation are more generally found in the Anglo-Saxon countries. This is because these forms of incentive regulations can easily be extended to non-economic objectives.

Performance-based regulation

Performance-based regulation (PBR), sometimes also called output regulation, basically ties retail prices – that is, the prices the infrastructure owner can charge to its users – to the achievement of particular objectives, set by the regulator. The two most common forms of PBR are award-penalty mechanisms (APMs) and multiyear rate plans (MRPs). In both cases, the goal is to incentivize the monopolist to develop new services as well as to increase his efficiency and productivity.

APMs aim to create incentives in particular areas. Typically, a key performance indicator (KPI) is chosen and defined by the regulator, who subsequently assesses its relative achievement by the regulated firm. Rates are then allowed to be adjusted by the regulated utility depending on the degree of achievement of the KPI. In principle, any indicators can be chosen, but usually the KPI pertains to reliability, timeliness, customer satisfaction, procurement costs, or some other factors. Again, a certain arbitrariness exists, be it in terms of choosing the KPI, setting the goal, and/or defining the allowed rate increase.

MRPs are a more widespread form of performance-based regulation. They typically are practiced by US-style utility regulators and rarely are applied to natural infrastructure monopolies. The idea is to engage into some sort of contract with the regulated firm over a certain period of time so as to mitigate against market fluctuations. This approach, sometimes also called "menu of contracts," allows for the inclusion of non-economic performance objectives, such as the development of renewables by electricity generators. The approach clearly fits into the toll good approach of US utilities regulators. There is also a link with the public-private-partnership contracts that we will see in the next chapter.

Both cases – APMs and MRPs – move away from simply regulating the pure monopoly in the European style and move toward supervising a more or less monopolistic firm in its price and product policy. This movement can be seen as a deviation from the narrowly defined role of an economic regulator to a broader social and even political role.

Benchmarking regulation

Benchmarking regulation, also sometimes called yardstick regulation, is yet another type of incentive regulation. Basically, benchmarking regulation compares the achievements of the regulated firm with the achievements of comparable competitors. Remuneration (that is, rates) is then tied to the *relative* achievement of objectives. Benchmarking removes some of the arbitrariness of target-setting by the regulator, yet the choice of the benchmarking companies remains somewhat arbitrary, inasmuch as totally comparable firms are often difficult to find given the monopolistic infrastructures.

"Sunshine regulation" is a weak form of benchmarking regulation in which no effective sanctioning mechanisms (for example, rate increases or decreases) are applied by the regulator. However, by comparing results (typically prices) among firms and exposing the results to the "sun," in other words to the press and the larger public, firms may be incentivized to do better.

Conclusion: when to use which regulation?

We have already seen that the use of the different regulatory approaches has a cultural dimension: while the continental European approach relies heavily on cost+ regulation, the Anglo-Saxon countries and regulators do have a certain preference for incentive-type regulation. But this also has to do with the fact that the US model of utilities regulation is not strictly economic (price-focused) and often includes other than purely financial objectives in its rate-making process. This US model also allows for a much more negoti-ated approach to regulation, something that is made possible because of the litigation allowed in the US judicial system.

Nevertheless, it is possible to establish some basic criteria when it comes to choosing the most appropriate type of regulation. Incentive regulation only makes sense when the results can be clearly observed and clearly attributed to the efforts made by the firm. If a firm's results will be heavily determined by its inherited infrastructure, for example, incentives (at least financial incentives) will be difficult to set, and cost+ regulation may be the better, or at least the fairer, option. The same goes for results that may be significantly determined by environmental factors upon which the regulated firm can have little impact, such as the weather or the overall economic situation. If the results can be clearly observed and the main portion of the results can be attributed to management action, some form of incentive regulation – from price-cap to performance-based regulations – may make sense. Benchmarking regulation only makes sense if the regulated firm, or at least some of its activities, can be compared with similar firms.

6 "Regulation by contract" – the French model

So far, I have presented two different approaches to the network industries: the US approach with its consequence of regulating utilities as toll goods and the EU approach consisting of unbundling competitive services from a regulated natural monopoly. But there is a third model, often called the "French model," which consists of tendering out monopolistic infrastructure services to private (and sometimes public) operators and subsequently establishing public-private partnerships between the mostly local authorities and these infrastructure service providers. In this French model, there is typically no regulation but the contract between the authority and the service provider; therefore, we can call this model "regulation by contract." As I will show in this chapter, regulation by contract is not a stable form of governance and will sooner or later be replaced by either US- or EU-style regulation.

There are different ways of looking at this French model: it can be seen as a precursor to the US model of utilities regulation, as an alternative to the US model, or as an intermediary step on the road from monopoly to competition. In any case, it is an alternative to the provision of traditional public services by State-Owned Enterprises (SOEs) or local public utilities. And this is how the French model started.

Origins of the French model

The original context of the French model is worthwhile to remember: France is a country of 37,000 municipalities, most of them too small to be able to provide public services, notably water and local transport. This situation led private companies to offer their services to operate monopolistic municipal infrastructures. Water services were the first to be outsourced by the municipalities to private operators, as early as the turn of the 20th century. Today, three big private operators provide water infrastructure services in most French municipalities.

During the 20th century, the model was extended to other municipal infrastructures, such as wastewater, waste management, and local public transport, and today encompasses many other things such as street lighting, services to the elderly, school buses, prisons, and many more. The list is by now almost limitless. And so are the modalities of the relationships between the municipalities and the service providers. Typically, this relationship takes the form of a sophisticated contract between the municipality and the service provider. In this contract, all the modalities, the objectives, the remunerations, the penalties, possible cancellations of the contract, and other features are "regulated" in detail.

As this contract is of a private nature, any breach of contract – by either side – will give rise to litigation and ultimately to a court decision. In this sense, the French model is more liberal than the US model of utilities regulation. But in terms of substance, it is quite similar: the services provided by the private operators are considered to be of a toll good nature (high rivalry but low excludability), which means that the contract looks at the services more in terms of a public than in terms of a private good. Unlike in the US case, where the state utilities regulator applies some standard principles to rate making, the French-type contract varies from one municipality to another, and there is a regulator who could apply at least some form of benchmarking.

Still, the model is considered to be quite successful, at least by some, as it allows even small municipalities to provide public services that they otherwise could not provide or that they could provide only at a much higher cost and/or with lesser quality. Others, especially from the left, criticize the model, arguing that the private sector should not be profiting from public services and from citizens who have no choice but to buy the services from the private monopolist.

From tendering to PPPs

Until the age of globalization (1980s, 1990s), this French model remained quite limited to France and its ex-colonies. But things changed in the context of liberalization. Suddenly, this French model came to be seen either as an alternative to privatization or as an intermediary step between the public monopoly and competitive markets. The operating firms, of course, saw the French model as an opportunity to grow their business. The World Bank played a key role in this process. Indeed, it theorized or at least conceptualized the approach, relabeled the French model as "public-private partnerships" (PPPs), elevated it from the local to the national level, and promoted it globally.

Competition for the market

While, in theory, competition was possible in the French model, competition was not put forward as being the hallmark of the model. What was mostly valued were the good and long-lasting relationships between the municipality and the operator of the infrastructure, thanks to which good public service could be guaranteed. As a consequence, most of the contracts were renewed with the same operators; when operators did change, the change was mostly due to the operators wanting to get out.

But this scenario changed in the context of liberalization. The firms operating under the French model, together with and with the help of the World Bank, looked for an alternative to the much more intrusive and less profitable EU model and the less intrusive but nevertheless regulated US model. In the context of the globalization of the 1980s and 1990s and the opening up of markets worldwide, many new investment opportunities appeared in developing and emerging countries, which the national governments could not stem. PPPs with mostly European firms appeared to be the most appropriate vehicle. It helped that, at the same time, so-called "structural adjustment programs" were put into place that forced these same countries to open up their public infrastructures for private investment (see financial PPPs, below).

Thus, the argument was developed that if competition in the market could not be created, one could at least have "competition for the market," a sort of "second-best liberalization solution." Neo-institutional economic theory provided the theoretical underpinning for this PPP approach. In reality, though, competition for the market means that the winner gets a monopoly for a certain time and has a strong chance to win again in the second and third rounds, considering the asymmetry of information between the incumbent and the new entrant.

In addition, and probably to avoid critical questioning, the World Bank created some sort of continuum from state-ownership via corporatization to PPPs to full privatization. This quite ideological continuum was, of course, intellectually flawed but had the advantage of making PPPs appear to be an intermediary step between monopolies and markets. Still, some sort of continuum can be constructed, but rather in terms of the degree of competition. This would be a continuum from the public monopoly in the form of an SOE (no competition), to competition for the market in its various forms (see below), to access competition EU-style, to, perhaps, full-fledged competition in the market. But whether things evolve this way will not so much depend upon the degree to which the state controls the assets (as is generally argued); rather, it will depend much more on the state of the technological development in that given sector. I will come back to this continuum in the conclusion of this book.

From competition for the market to PPPs

How does competition for the market work, and how do we get from there to PPPs? This process can be described in four steps: in a first step, a confined, generally local, sometimes regional, but rarely national monopoly is put up for tender for a specified period of time (see below for a typology of PPPs). In a second step, private or sometimes even public firms (utilities) bid; that is, submit an offer for that monopoly. In the case of heavy public service burdens, the offer may actually entail the request for a subsidy. Also, the tender (as well as the bid and the award criteria) is typically comprehensive and entails both financial and non-financial (for example, quality of service, public service obligations) elements. In a third step, the tendering (public) authority (municipal, city, or regional but rarely national government) selects the "best" offer using pre-specified award criteria. This selection can imply receiving money from or paying money (subsidies) to the bidder. In a fourth step, all this is translated into a contract between the public authority and the winner of the tender. This contract "regulates" the relationship between the two parties; that is, it specifies their respective responsibilities and rights, including the monitoring of its execution. From a theoretical point of view, this contract reflects a typical principal-agent problem.

Typology of PPPs

There are as many PPPs as there are contracts; each contract is different, designed to the specific situation. Nevertheless, over time, a certain typology of PPPs has emerged, not the least because the World Bank needed a taxonomy to assess risks and opportunities for the firms interested in engaging in PPPs. The most basic distinction is between "management PPPs" and "financial PPPs."

Management PPPs typically come about when infrastructures already exist. The public authorities offer the "management" of the infrastructure, for example, water pipes, for tender. Over time, three such types of tender or contract have emerged. The main difference is the duration of the contract, which in turn is a function of how much risk the contracting party is willing to take and how much control the public authority is willing to release:

- "Management contracts" typically have a duration of three to five years: the private (or public) operator takes on the management of the infrastructure (the water pipes, to stick with our example), yet the ownership of the infrastructure (the water pipes), the long-term financing, the working capital, and even the proceeds of selling the water remain with the public authority.

- "Lease contracts" (also called "affermage")[1] typically have a duration from 6 to 15 years: here the private operator takes on the management of the infrastructure and also collects the proceeds of his work (that is, the price the customers pay for the water). Quite logically, he also provides the working capital. Yet the ownership of the assets as well as the long-term financing remain with the public authority.
- "Concession contracts" (15+ years) differ from affermage in that the private operator also provides the long-term financing of the infrastructure. The ownership of the assets, at least on paper, always remains with the public authority; that is where a PPP differs from full-fledged privatization.

Financial PPPs differ from management PPPs inasmuch as the infrastructure does not exist to begin with. The private firm – more typically a consortium of firms combining financiers, builders, and an operator – thus brings the long-term financing (the investments needed), constructs the infrastructure, and operates it thereafter. A typical example is toll roads, as well as airports, homes for the elderly, and prisons. One can distinguish between two types of financial PPP:

- In BOT (build-operate-transfer) PPPs, as the name implies, the private firm builds the airport, operates the airport, and transfers the assets of the airport to the public authority at the expiration of the concession, which can be a minimum of 15 years but typically is longer.
- In BTO (build-transfer-operate) PPPs, on the other hand, the private firm transfers the assets to the public authorities right after constructing the airport, bridge, or tunnel, for example. In exchange for having invested and constructed the infrastructure, the consortium will typically receive a concession contract (15–99 years) or sometimes a lease contract (6–15 years), which gives it the right to operate the infrastructure and collect proceeds and, by doing so, recuperate the investments plus make a profit.

Which of the two financial PPP models is chosen is again a function of risk distribution between the private operator (the consortium) and the public authority: the riskier the investment, the more likely there will be a BTO.

PPPs are here to stay

PPPs are quite controversial. But controversy varies depending on the sectors: as a matter of rule, the more public service obligations are involved, the more controversial the PPP. The critique comes mainly from the left, which argues that public services, such as water, prisons, police, or the military, should not be outsourced to the private sector, as the private sector is basically after money, which in turn creates wrong incentives (for example, more prisoners, more wars, or more water consumption).

Assessment of PPPs

While the above critique stating that PPPs set wrong incentives in the case of public services is certainly valid, PPPs also have benefits. Private and especially big private operators bring expertise, professionalism, and international standards to the table. The quality of the resulting services is generally better than when the services are provided by small public operators. Also, big companies that manage several PPPs in a given sector can generate economies of scale and make efficiency gains. Regulation must ensure that these efficiency gains are passed on to the public sector and ultimately to the customer, however. Big firms specializing in PPPs in a given sector are generally more innovative and apply state-of-the-art technologies.

On the negative side, services provided by way of PPPs are generally more expensive than if they were provided by the public sector, the difference typically being the dividends that the private operators have to return to their shareholders. Although less tangible, PPPs tend to shift the risks to the public sector, something that often only becomes visible once things go wrong. Problems occur with social equity or cream-skimming; that is, private operators tending to service the high-paying customers more readily than the less lucrative ones. Also, the longer the PPP lasts, the more the in-house expertise moves to the private sector, a condition that is well known in theory as the asymmetry of information problem. This, in turn, can create a so-called lock-in with the private partner. Finally, PPPs incentivize corruption, given that the bidding firm can obtain a long-term monopoly and therefore might be willing to be the authority that puts out the tender. Only strong institutional capacity and ultimately strong regulation is capable of withstanding these negative aspects of PPPs.

Contextual forces

Despite these criticisms, there are several very strong contextual forces that make PPPs more or less unavoidable in the medium and long term. The most important one is the growing scarcity of public funds. As we have seen, network industries are capital intensive ("asset specific" in the terminology of new institutional economics). Yet the public sector increasingly encounters financial problems because nation-states, sub-national regions, cities, and municipalities are put into competition with one another because of globalization. In many cases, only the private sector has the financial capability to fund big infrastructure investments. This condition is even more true for mega-projects. In this case, PPPs, especially financial PPPs, often appear as the only possible answer.

The same argument holds for the growing lack of expertise available in the public sector, which again is due in large part to its financial problems. But this lack of public sector expertise is also due to the ever more sophisticated and dynamic technological nature of the infrastructures. Municipalities, and especially small municipalities, now rarely have the expertise to run technologically advanced water treatment plants or sophisticated mobility services, for example.

A third contextual force pertains to the rise of global firms that have specialized in PPPs. These firms include the traditional French water, transport, and construction firms but also many construction and especially infrastructure firms from emerging countries, especially from China. In other words, not only does the public sector increasingly need private partners, but firms whose business model relies entirely on concession contracts with the public sector are increasingly competent and also increasingly aggressive at a global scale.

In this sense, the French model has now become a global model. It has extended from local PPPs to big national infrastructure projects. And these projects are becoming more and more multi-sectoral: no longer are PPPs about only water or wastewater, for example; they now encompass bundles of infrastructure services (for example, water, wastewater, waste, and even mobility) and take totally new forms, such as PPPs to build entire "smart private cities." All this evolution leads to an urgent need for regulation.

The growing need for regulation

Considering the proportions that PPPs are taking – both in terms of complexity and in terms of financial volume – and considering that the "partnership" has become ever more unequal (for example, small municipalities versus big multinationals), "regulating" PPPs simply by contract will no longer suffice. Yet it is not entirely clear how such regulation could or should look in the future. Applying US-style utility regulation to PPPs would be relatively easy to do, as the spirit of the French-model PPP and the spirit of US-style utility regulation are quite similar. However, this regulation would create some incompatibilities with EU-style, sector-specific regulation. Whether or not a new and specific regulatory approach to the spreading PPPs should and will be developed will very much depend upon their prevalence in the future and even more so upon the problems that they generate.

Note

1 The word comes from the French word "farm" and means that the management of the farmland is leased out (by contract) to a farmer who does not own the farm but operates it typically for a 6- to 15-year period.

7   Post and telecom

In this chapter, I present the liberalization of both the postal and telecommunications sectors. The reason both are treated in the same chapter stems from the fact that in all countries, except the United States, post and telecom were initially integrated in the same SOE, called PTT (Post, Telegraph, Telecom). The order of the words is important since post was the first network industry ever, with roots back to the empires of Persia and Rome.

Postal services were successfully developed by medieval city-states in Europe and typically operated by private operators. With the emergence of the modern nation-states in the 18th and 19th centuries, postal services became nationalized, considering their foundational economic function. During the second half of the 19th century, the telegraph emerged; telephony emerged toward the end of the 19th century. Since both were also communications infrastructures, they were simply integrated into the postal services, thus PTT. Only in the United States did telephony quickly become a private monopoly (AT&T, or American Telegraph and Telephone), whereas the US Postal Service become the only federal, public enterprise, which it remains today.

Telegraphy died somewhere after the second World War, but PTTs continued to exist up to the liberalization of the 1990s. At that time, PTTs were split up into telecoms and posts, the reason being that, with emerging competition (see below), the telecom part could no longer afford to cross-subsidize the postal part. Also, postal services worldwide – at least the ones without financial postal services, about 50 percent – started to lose money as of the 1950s. In some cases, governments sold off their national telecommunications operators and sometimes also their postal banking services to the private sector.

Postal services

Postal services are the oldest network industry and as such are not really the result of some technological innovation or even revolution, as are railways or electricity, for example. Their value chain is thus very simple: mail items (letters and parcels) are brought by the paying sender to a collection point (letter box, post office); these items are then transported to a sorting center and from there fed into a distribution network. The national public enterprise – the PTT and, after the 1990s, the post – owns and controls the entire value chain and had, until the 1990s, not only a legal but also a de facto monopoly over both letters and parcels.

Strong economic reasons existed for the postal monopoly, the most important being the direct network effects that are typical for two-sided markets: indeed, postal operators are simply mediators between senders, who can also be receivers, and receivers, who can also be senders. In this sense, postal services are precursors of "platforms" and display corresponding network effects: the more senders, the better it is for the receivers, and vice versa. There are also significant economies of scale, especially in letter mail distribution. Indeed, the mail person walks or drives his/her delivery tour no matter how many mail items there are. Consequently, marginal costs are very low, just as in all other network industries. Finally, there are also economies of density, again especially in the distribution part of the value chain: the more densely populated the area, the lower the unit costs.

Besides these purely economic characteristics, the postal sector has some other noteworthy features: unlike in all other network industries, technology did not play a significant role in the postal sector until the 1990s, when automatization started, and especially the 2010s, when digitalization fully hit posts. No major monopolistic infrastructure exists in postal services, which means there are hardly any entry barriers, except for the above-mentioned network effects. Finally, the postal sector is highly politicized, owing both to its public service mission and to its labor intensity. Posts were and sometimes still are the biggest national employers.

Liberalization

Liberalization in the postal sector started out in a de facto manner and not all as a result of explicit liberalization policies: because of globalization, nationally focused postal operators had a hard time responding to new, global postal needs (such as courier services), which opened the way for companies such as FedEx, United Parcel Services (UPS), and DHL. DHL has since been bought by Deutsche Post. As there were no monopolistic infrastructures, de facto liberalization simply took the form of duplicating the value chain.

Subsequently, the European Union followed suit and engaged, during the second half of the 1990s, in a stepwise liberalization process by which the legal monopoly of the historical postal operators was gradually reduced to

350 grams; to 100 grams; to 50 grams; and, as of 2013, to zero. Since then, the European postal market has been fully open for competition.

In the United States, the situation is different; the US Postal Service still enjoys an effective monopoly over the distribution part of letter mail. But overall, postal operators are now basically competing in all services, namely financial services if they still exist; parcels, where postal operators have lost generally over 50 to 70 percent of their market share; and letters. Yet postal operators remain dominant market players in letter mail, namely because of the economies of scale, but also because the market is rapidly shrinking, owing to electronic substitution. A few postal operators have recently been fully or at least partly privatized.

Regulation

There is little to be regulated in the postal services after liberalization. This is somewhat paradoxical as sector-specific postal regulators had been created (on the model of telecom regulators) by the Second European Postal Directive (1996), were copied in most countries, and have not been abolished since. Still, the only thing left to regulate is the so-called Universal Services Obligation (USO), which hardly justifies the existence of a postal regulator. In theory, the USO could be tendered and provided by any competing postal operator but in practice always ends up with the incumbent. Typically, the USO remains a burden for the incumbent, as the USO has not adapted to the digital age (for example, distribution of shrinking mail volumes to every household often still occurs every day) and is generally not remunerated. All the regulator does in the matter of USO regulation is ensure that the incumbent complies with USO standards.

Future challenges

The postal sector was the first network industry, but it may also be the first one to disappear. Postal financial services are still a business in some countries where posts have managed to turn into banks (for example, Japan, France, Italy), but basically postal financial services are a thing of the past. Parcels are seeing huge growth rates due to Internet-fueled global e-commerce. But most of these parcels do not end up with incumbents, as incumbents remain focused on their national markets. E-commerce is therefore mainly profiting the big global players. In that global parcel business, there is also a huge consolidation going on, mainly due to fierce competition. Furthermore, digital platforms, such as Amazon and Alibaba, are themselves entering the parcel distribution business, thus incorporating the cost of distribution directly into their products (for example, "free" distribution).

While digitalization is fueling and consolidating the global parcel business, the letter business is rapidly being substituted by electronic communication (first email and now social media). In the most digitally advanced countries, mail volumes have already been halved and continue to decline. Letter mail has remained mainly national, with incumbents dominating the respective national markets. The future of the incumbents in the postal sector is thus quite bleak.

Telecommunications

Telecommunications follow quite logically from the postal services. As said above, they were integrated into PTTs at the end of the 19th century and then emancipated themselves about a century later. The value chain of telecommunications is even simpler than that of posts: transmission between the caller and the receiver. Both the caller and the receiver pay.

Before and even during the early phases of telecom liberalization, only copper cables served as the transmission infrastructure. About ten years into the liberalization process, mobile telephony emerged as a result of a major technological revolution. This in turn changed the course of telecom liberalization. Technological developments in wireless communications are extremely rapid, moving from the first-generation technology (1G) to now 5G. Significant technological developments in fixed telephony have also occurred, notably with fiber technology, introduced in the beginning of the 21st century. However, the value chain and the business models of the telecommunications operators did not change much until recently.

Like in the postal sector, strong direct network effects led to and justified the monopolistic nature of telecommunications. Economies of scale (much bigger than in the postal sector due to their heavy infrastructure investments) enhanced the telecommunication operators' monopolies. This latter characteristic was somewhat relaxed in the case of mobile telephony, as market entry became much easier due to the much lower sunk costs. Yet direct network effects remained the same and are a strong consideration in the attribution of mobile telephony frequencies: as frequencies are limited, a sufficient amount of them need to be allocated to an operator for network effects to be effective. This, in turn, limits the amount of mobile telephony operators in a given country, typically to three or four.

Liberalization

Prior to the liberalization of the telecommunications sector in the 1990s in Europe, the breakup of AT&T, the US private monopoly, occurred in 1982 by the US antitrust authority. This breakup led to several US regional monopolies, which were allowed to compete against each other. More importantly, it also led to a company (AT&T) whose only focus was international telephony and who consequently started to attack the European market, thus triggering EU liberalization. In the same context of growing competitive pressure on European operators, the privatization of British Telecom (BT, now Vodaphone) must also be mentioned.

Telecommunications liberalization was initiated by the European Commission back when only fixed telephony existed. Thus, liberalization followed and actually initiated the typical model of unbundling and access to the unbundled infrastructure: competing telecom operators were to be enabled to access the cable infrastructure of the incumbent and sell telephony services directly to consumers. This liberalization model was subsequently applied by the commission to the other infrastructures, notably electricity, gas, and rail. Paradoxically, full institutional unbundling as a means to telecommunications liberalization never happened; instead, mobile telephony emerged as an alternative to fixed telephony, and incumbent telecom operators successfully lobbied against their unbundling by stating that competition from mobile operators amounted to a form of "infrastructure competition," which made unbundling obsolete.

Quite logically then, in 2002, a major shift occurred in telecommunications regulation, whereby the sector-specific approach to regulation was replaced by competition regulation, meaning that incumbent telecom operators were now scrutinized for their dominance in specific market segments. Yet at the institutional level, things stayed the same, and national, sector-specific telecom regulators were now tasked with competition regulation-type work. In addition, their work also encompassed the attribution of spectrum licenses.

Future challenges

Telecommunications – transmission of information and now also of data – is characterized by rapid technological change, not just in transmission technology but also in the adjacent fields of data generation, data analysis, and data display. Therefore, regulation of the telecommunications sector also has to evolve rapidly, and probably in directions that are difficult to anticipate. The following two developments have triggered new regulatory considerations but have not yet led to profoundly new regulatory approaches.

OTT (for "over-the-top") means that traditional voice telephony is increasingly being substituted by Internet telephony, as provided by Skype, WhatsApp, or Viber, for example. This leads to the type of regulatory questions I will address in the last chapter of the book, namely questions about the regulation of "digital platforms," as well as about regulation regarding the remuneration of the physical (telephony and other) infrastructures by such digital platforms. These new services and now platforms undermine the very business models of the traditional infrastructure providers, notably telecommunications operators. Originally, this development only threatened the business models of the incumbents, but today new entrants in mobile telephony are also threatened.

This challenge leads directly to the second regulatory challenge for telecommunications operators, namely their vertical integration. As a strategic reaction to being used by platform providers, in particular digital content providers (movies, news, radio, etc.), telecommunications operators – both incumbents and new entrants – have ventured into the same business as their competitors, yet they are building on their own telecom infrastructure as a competitive advantage. Consequently, they are bundling telephony and Internet access services (increasingly flat-rate Internet access services) together with content. This has triggered the so-called "net neutrality" debate, whereby regulators are requested by the content providers to prohibit such bundling and force telecom operators and Internet access providers to be "neutral"; that is, not to discriminate vis-à-vis content. This debate is still going on and has, in the context of digital platforms, also moved to other infrastructures, as we will see later.

8 Transport

In this chapter on transport, I discuss mostly railways and air transport, as they are the most interesting transport sectors in terms of de- and re-regulation. Maritime transport is, of course, also a network industry and in certain respects quite similar to air transport. Sometimes road transport, either for passengers or for freight, is also referred to as a network industry. But both are de facto already liberalized and intellectually less challenging. I will briefly discuss these three network industries at the end of this chapter.

Transportation is interesting because it is going through rapid transformations, owing notably to automatization and digitalization. As a result, the various transport modes are less and less clearly separable, a phenomenon known as "multimodality" and observable both in logistics and even more so in passenger transport. This multimodality is why, in a third section, I also present urban, public transport for passengers to illustrate how transport is about to evolve and will have to be regulated in the future.

Railways

Railways are the result of a profound technological revolution – the steam engine – combined with rapid industrial development at the end of the 19th century in the United Kingdom, the United States, and continental Europe, as well as the Ottoman Empire and Russia. Although the very first rail development initiatives were private, railways rapidly became nationalized at the turn of the century, except in the United States, as they were considered essential for national development and defense. After the Second World War, trucks and cars rapidly became an alternative to the train, and the modal share of the railways declined; most countries that had not had railways developed by their colonizers did not invest in this heavy and expensive technology. Because of both environmental reasons and, mostly, congestion, a revival of railways is occurring, especially in the high-speed sector. Japan and France led the way, followed by Italy, Spain, and emerging countries, notably China and Korea. The railway industry is most developed in Europe, where networks are dense and have historically developed over time. In addition, Russia, India, China, Korea, and Japan are highly developed railway countries.

Railway characteristics

The railway value chain is quite straightforward: passengers enter a station, board a train, are transported via an infrastructure (tracks and signals), and exit at another station. The same goes for freight, which uses different charging and discharging stations, yet typically travels in trains run on the same tracks as the passenger trains, with ensuing operational problems. In the beginning of the railways, the main countries using them had their own suppliers, notably the main European countries such as France, Germany, and Switzerland.

Economically, railways are a typical network industry with strong direct network effects: the more developed the network, the better for every user. But more importantly, railways also display very strong economies of scale, resulting mainly from the high sunk costs of the railway infrastructure (tracks and stations), as well as of the rolling stock. Network effects are further reinforced because of the high technical complementarities between the rolling stock and the infrastructure, mainly due to historical reasons; that is, the highly national and national supplier-driven nature of railways. In other words, as is still true today, only certain trains can run on certain tracks. Changing this fact is one of the major changes that will have to take place in the process of railways' liberalization.

In addition, railways display many political characteristics: they are highly subsidized, probably the most subsidized among all the network industries, in part because railways are simply an expensive technology but also because of intermodal competition from trucks and private cars. Typically, railway companies are strong national actors (in the countries that have railways), and they have all the in-house capabilities to make the railway system work. Railways generally also have numerous public service obligations that make them subject to political interference. Except in some emerging countries, where governments invest, railways are often in debt, in part because of their non-lucrative public service obligations and lack of restructuring after the boom of the automobile industry.

Liberalization

Railway liberalization is mainly, if not exclusively, a European endeavor: as a matter of fact, the European Commission (EC) took on railway liberalization before telecommunications liberalization, with the disappointing result that, as of today, railways are hardly liberalized. Railway liberalization was actually preceded by railway privatization in the United Kingdom and some form of liberalization in Sweden. The EC took on some of these ideas but had a much more ambitious plan, namely to create a single European railway area, where trains could run freely across a European network (infrastructure) and where train operating companies (TOCs, both passenger and freight) would compete against each other, thanks to advances in interoperability. This approach, called "access competition," was indeed the original model, and many regulations were made in light of this, notably interoperability and access rules (see below). The TOCs would own and operate their own trains (locomotives and wagons) and sell train services directly to their customers. They would not face any major obstacles when wanting to offer their services on any given track in any given European country. Infrastructure managers (IMs) would do the network planning and make investment decisions, construct and maintain the network, and grant access to the TOCs on a non-discriminatory basis, depending on the availability of slots. To this effect, the big national train operators would have to be unbundled. Railway stations could either belong to the IM or be businesses on their own but, in any case, would also have to grant non-discriminatory access to the TOCs.

This vision is not how things turned out and is unlikely to materialize. Even though in freight transport the EC managed to liberalize the market by way of access competition, in passenger rail the increasingly dominant model is the so-called franchise competition. Indeed, for passenger rail access, competition remains limited to certain lucrative lines between cities with high passenger volumes and is almost non-existent in high-speed rail (with the exception of Italy), even though it is still actively promoted by the EC. Big national railway companies, such as SNCF (France), Deutsche Bahn (Germany), and Ferrovie dello Stato (Italy), are not totally unbundled, but this is not the main reason why there is little access competition in passenger transport. The main reason is the absence of lucrative rail business and lack of interest from competitors on most of the network. Where rail can be a lucrative business, namely on some intercity lines and in mass transit in densely populated urban areas, access competition is made difficult because of congestion.

As stated previously, the dominant model of railway liberalization has become franchise competition, whereby a public authority – either a central or regional government – tenders franchises; that is, the exclusive right for a train operator to exclusively serve a given geographical area during a certain period of time. Typically, the franchisee uses the infrastructure and pays a fee. Most of the time, the franchisee also owns the rolling stock, but sometimes even the rolling stock belongs to the public authority. Franchisees generally also receive a subsidy for providing public services or must cross-subsidize some non-lucrative public services from the profits they make on their lucrative lines. This franchise system must be heavily regulated to function.

Regulation

Not astonishingly, economic railway regulators were created early on by the EC in all member states. Also, the European Railway Agency (ERA) emerged, mainly to promote safety and interoperability standards. As of today, railway regulation mainly pertains to the three following areas (Finger and Messulam, 2015):

- The most important area is the non-discriminatory access to the rail infrastructure by the different TOCs. This access has come to include non-discriminatory access to the passenger railway and to the cargo charging stations. Furthermore, timetable construction and real-time slot allocation have emerged as areas where discrimination can and does occur. In a totally unbundled railway system, timetables and slot allocation can be the task of the IM, but if unbundling is not perfect, slot allocation requires much heavier regulatory oversight.
- The second most important area of regulation is access charges, which, according to EU directives, are to cover the "directly incurred costs as result of operating the service." Calculating these directly incurred costs is more easily said than done, considering the different types of trains, the various degrees of congestion of the system, and many other factors. A high potential of discrimination related to access charges exists, especially in the case of still vertically integrated railway companies.
- The third most important area of railway regulation pertains to franchises and is even more complicated than the first two. Franchises are regulated as a type of toll good where economic and social considerations are combined, given the public services nature of most franchises. Therefore, regulation must consider the problem of cross-subsidization, both from the lucrative part of the franchise to the non-lucrative part and inversely when it comes to the use of public subsidies for private market developments. As the United Kingdom is the most advanced country in terms of franchising railways, the UK regulator – the Office of Road and Rail (ORR) – has probably developed the best expertise in this area.

Future challenges

The future challenges of the railway industry are huge and cannot be addressed by market mechanisms alone. Considering past public investment in roads, cheap fuel prices, and more recent intermodal competition, exacerbated by digitalization (see below), rail can hardly compete and therefore must be considered, before all, as a public policy instrument. Its main aim is to provide efficient and environmentally more sustainable mobility services, especially in densely populated areas (as mass transit) and in between major urban areas. This rail service has costs, and government must be ready to invest in infrastructure development, maintenance, and sometimes even rolling stock. Government must also be ready, at least in some countries, to be willing to close down unprofitable lines that are probably better and more efficiently serviced by buses and other road-based mobility providers.

Competition in this highly subsidized and technologically complex system will never develop to the point the EC originally envisioned. While competition will certainly establish itself in freight, similar competition in long-distance railways and even high-speed rail may or may not appear, depending on political pressure. Franchise competition for regional and even certain urban railway lots will also further develop. However, a technical limitation to competition exists, in addition to economic limitations; competition in highly congested systems (for example, the Netherlands, Switzerland, London, Paris) makes little sense and generates inefficiencies and unnecessary regulatory costs.

Air transport

Air transport is the only network industry that, historically, has always been unbundled: airports were, and still are to a large extent, locally owned; air traffic control (ATC) is a national, public monopoly; and airlines, with the exception of those in the United States, were national, publicly owned so-called flag carriers. All three parts of air transport form a single infrastructure system, as none can operate without the others (Finger and Button, 2017).

Consequently, the value chain of air transport is very similar to that of the rail and maritime sectors: passengers (or freight) enter an airport, travel by plane, and exit at another airport. Taking off, overflight, and landing is made possible by ATC, or more precisely air traffic management (ATM). ATM, in turn, performs several functions, the most important being the allocation of airspace (planning), as well as separating aircraft from one another. Suppliers are also part of the broad air transport industry; especially in the early years of aviation, several countries had their own suppliers (e.g., the

Netherlands, Sweden), but with liberalization and standardization a concentration process has taken place, leading to only two dominant suppliers remaining today, Airbus and Boeing.

Direct network effects exist in the airline segment of the air transport industry, which is how "network airlines" came to exist. But such economic forces are strongly limited, mainly because of overriding safety concerns and, even more importantly, the national nature of air transport. Indeed, network effects – which should be global to deploy their full power – are limited by the so-called Chicago Convention of 1944, which puts the authority to fly into the hands of bilateral agreements between governments. Even though any airline could in principle fly everywhere, governments decide who gets to fly where and when.

Air transport is otherwise still quite politicized: ATC has a strong military component, which limits its liberalization. ATC is also strongly unionized, which has prevented its evolution until recently. And airports are often strongly influenced by local politics, either because airports can be money makers, they are instruments of local development, or both. Even though air transport portrays itself as a highly dynamic and liberalized network industry, this description is only true in certain countries (the United States, China) and in certain geographical areas, such as Europe and more recently Asia. As a matter of fact, the EU has become the model for air transport liberalization.

Liberalization

It is important to understand how liberalization works in the airline segment of the air transport industry, namely as a stepwise, gradual relaxation of the so-called airline freedoms, as defined by the Chicago Convention: legally determining from which airport in a given country each airline may fly, to which airport in another country (plus overflying one or more third countries). In the case of Europe, we have an open internal market as of 1993, whereby any EU-registered airline can fly from any EU airport to any other EU airport, provided it finds take-off and landing slots. This open market has given rise to powerful low-cost companies. This rise of the low-cost airlines and subsequent significant air traffic growth is indeed the success story of EU air transport liberalization. EU liberalization had been preceded by the United States (1978), where, among other factors, the regulation of tariffs and timetables was relaxed and even abandoned, creating an internal US market. In the EU context, sales and reservation systems were also unbundled from the airlines, allowing for price comparisons and more competition among airlines.

Another significant area of air transport liberalization, first in Europe and now worldwide, is the unbundling and liberalization of airport services, such as ground handling, approach and tarmac operations, tarmac services, and real estate. This unbundling has led to franchise competition at many airports and the rise of dedicated airport operations firms (both public and private). Airports, after all, are the most lucrative segments of the air transport industry.

ATC remains a public monopoly, mainly for safety but also for national security reasons. The fact that ATC is still very much in the hands of unions does not help ATC liberalization, either. Besides airport charges and slots, ATC – that is, the transformation of the national, public air navigation service providers (ANSPs) and the creation of a so-called Single European Sky in the case of Europe – is the next big challenge in air transport liberalization and regulation.

Regulation

There is plenty of regulation in the air transport sector with safety regulations permeating the entire sector. The most liberalized part of air transport is the airlines, but even here, plenty of regulation prevails. The EU is in this respect a global exception and a forerunner, as the EU approach is difficult to replicate in other regions given the absence of supranational organizations. Indeed, only in the EU have air transport freedoms been abandoned altogether. Of course, countries can liberalize their airline markets domestically, which can significantly affect traffic growth in countries with a significant internal market, such as China, India, Russia, and Mexico. But in between countries, liberalization hinges on bilateral agreements and, in the case of the EU, agreements between a national government and the EC. Another unique feature of EU regulation is its regulation of passenger rights.

As for airports, many regulations pertain to operations and are safety or security related (for example, tarmac operations or ground handling, respectively). From an economic point of view, regulation mainly pertains to airport charges and airport slots. Both are typically regulated at a local level, even though national governments and the EU are trying to put some sound economic analysis into a system that is dominated both by local politics and by a very complicated relationship between airports and airlines. Typically, airports are local monopolies, with competition among airports only existing in some big cities. But it is not always clear who dominates: if the airport is mainly used by a big flag-carrier (or a low-cost airline, for that matter) (for example airports, such as Frankfurt, Paris Charles de Gaulle, London-Luton), airports may have little freedom to set charges. In the cases where airport usage is diversified, airports may have power over airlines. A complicated relationship also exists between the costs of operating an airport, which should be paid by the airlines, and the profits made by the airport thanks to duty-free and other shopping-related incomes, something that has become known as the "single till versus dual till" problem. Big regulatory challenges await here.

Another big liberalization and regulation challenge yet to come involves airport slots. Along with airspace over congested regions such as Europe, China, and the United States, airport slots are *the* scarce resource that now hinders air traffic growth. Airlines are able to conserve their airport slots because of their so-called grandfather rights. Auction mechanisms are being explored, and the EU is trying to create some regulation, but auctioning is difficult because airlines need pairs of slots, with the second slot of the pair possibly being anywhere in the world.

As for ATC, charges are set by national governments and regulated. More recently, the EC introduced a very sophisticated and, in regulatory terms, heavy-handed performance scheme, aimed at harmonizing ATC charges. However, the EU started a far-reaching initiative called Single European Sky (SES) in 1999 to try not only to harmonize but also to integrate the European sky, to make air transport seamless. As things are moving very slowly, new approaches of unbundling ATM are being explored, whereby some unbundled services could be liberalized. Three basic types of service compose ATM, namely airspace management, air traffic services, and air traffic flow management, and some of them could be provided competitively. But the road to the SES is still long and is so far limited to Europe.

Challenges

Because of the liberalization of the airline segment of the air transport industry and because of the leading role of the EU, air transport has become quite dynamic, even though this dynamism has stalled somewhat recently because of market concentration and national politics. Yet at the same time, technology is moving rapidly, providing a new impetus to the air transport sector.

Indeed, competition among airlines has led to substantial market concentration and to the subsequent disappearance of many airlines. In parallel, some big, low-cost airlines have emerged. On the supplier side, market concentration is even bigger. And we clearly see that in markets where competition has stalled – especially in the United States – prices have risen, and service quality has decreased. As a consequence, the further development of passenger rights may well become a necessity, as it is unclear how economic regulation could prevent further global market concentration. Also, the airline market is significantly distorted by geopolitically inspired airline policies, for example, in the case of the Gulf carriers or in the US market, which is still not open to international competition. It is also distorted by local, national, and global policies in terms of subsidies for airports, especially new, big, global hubs.

New, big challenges for the air transport sector stem from technological changes, namely automatization and digitalization. Unmanned Automated Vehicles (UAVs, also called drones) might substantially disrupt air transport, especially ATM. Already more drones are in the air than airplanes, which is bound to become a safety and a capacity problem very soon. It is obvious that ATM can no longer continue as in the past and will have to change profoundly. A possible way out (or not) may be offered by satellite navigation and digital communications, whereby both manned and unmanned planes would communicate directly with each other. This scenario in turn would lead to unprecedented regulatory challenges, which current governments and regulators could not handle. The EU is addressing this challenge as part of its SES initiative and will probably play a leading role globally.

Finally, the elephant in the air transport room is global warming: while the air transport sector's contribution to global CO_2 emissions is somewhat limited compared to that of other transport modes (road and especially maritime), airplane emissions at high altitudes have additional climate forcing effects. Environmental regulations, including caps on air traffic, will at some point start to affect the air transport industry.

Urban public transport

No urban public transport industry exists, and even less so an urban public transport network industry. However, urban public transport – and increasingly urban private transport – has become the most dynamic portion of the transport industry, though not necessarily in terms of liberalization but rather in terms of technological innovation (Finger and Auduoin, 2018). The backdrop of such innovation is rapid urbanization everywhere: urban agglomerations become ever bigger, reaching far beyond traditional city, regional, and even national jurisdictions. People commute ever longer distances to work, and most of the transport is done by private cars in industrialized countries and by all kinds of mostly private buses in emerging and developing countries. This commuting leads to unprecedented pollution and congestion and huge losses of productivity and quality of life. A similar evolution can be observed when it comes to urban logistics.

The urban transport challenges

Urban and especially regional, agglomerated public transportation is highly fragmented in terms of connections between transport modes and administrative jurisdictions. Typically, mass transit trains are operated by national public railway companies in a monopolistic manner. Local, monopolistic metro, bus, BRT (bus rapid transit), and tram services exist, often not crossing administrative and political boundaries, even though people cross these jurisdictions daily. In addition, regulated local taxi services (concessions) operate. Increasingly, one finds Uber-type private services, private and public bike sharing systems, and all kinds of other innovative transport offerings.

Clearly, urban public and private transport is not a network industry, even though huge direct network effects, economies of scale, and economies of density would occur if it were. But these network effects cannot be achieved because of jurisdictional, ownership, interconnection, and interoperability problems. In short, urban transport contains enormous yet untapped efficiency potential. To make things even more complicated and inefficient, many elements of urban public transport are subsidized or regulated in incoherent ways. Markets would certainly exist, but it is unclear how they could develop given all this fragmentation and administrative, political, regulatory, and financing incoherence. Market entry is difficult, which is where liberalization and digitalization come in.

Liberalization and digitalization

Uneven liberalization exists in urban public transport, which further contributes to its fragmentation. Mass transit is typically not liberalized and could at best be franchised. The same is true for metros, trams, and BRT. Some cities do franchise some lines, but cities rarely franchise their entire public transport system to one single operator. Bus routes are more typically franchised to private operators, but their planning, timetables, and ticketing is typically coordinated at the municipal level. As described in the chapter on PPPs, cities use various possibilities to bring in private partners to operate bits and pieces of their public transport system. Cities license taxi companies, while new entrants such as Uber-type services enter the urban agglomeration, often beginning without any license. The result is a patchwork of services without an integrated public transport offering, such as interconnected services, integrated timetables, or especially integrated ticketing. For many cities and especially urban agglomerations, integration is almost impossible to achieve, even with strong political will, as transport generally goes beyond the political limits of a city.

This is where digitalization comes in: indeed, digitalization turns out to be the most active driver of urban transport liberalization, as digital platforms can offer route planning as well as price and service comparisons across transport modes and transport operators. Digital platforms are also not limited to administrative and political jurisdictions. Most digital urban mobility platforms are still at an early stage, but one can already anticipate their potential to redefine the urban public and private transport landscape. What's unclear is whether, without regulation, this evolution will lead to a more coherent public transportation system that ultimately serves the needs of the majority of the users and of the urban agglomeration.

Regulation and future challenges

At present, each urban transport mode is regulated separately, some at the local, some at the regional, and some at the national level, if they are regulated at all. In many cities, urban transport authorities have emerged, but their role mostly relates to planning and sometimes licensing. Urban transport regulation has not developed much yet, and it is not clear how it should or could be developed, as urban agglomerations and metropolitan areas have no jurisdictional authority to regulate. I see in particular two challenges for such regulation – intermodality and digitalization:

• Urban public and private transport is foremost a challenge of intermodality: the different modes of transport must be considered in relationship with and in complementarity to one another, not separately. How to execute intermodal planning, coordination, and even ticketing, regulating the different transport modes so that a seamless transport journey results, is far from obvious.
• Before this problem of regulating intermodality can be tackled in a systematic way, digital platforms will already have emerged in urban areas and take on this coordinating role. Then the regulation of intermodality will very rapidly evolve into a regulation of digital mobility platforms. I will discuss the regulation of such mobility and other platforms in Chapter 10.

At the urban level, economic considerations are being, and increasingly will be, overtaken by public policy concerns and objectives pertaining to public service, congestion, air pollution, CO_2 emissions, and quality of life, among others. All this will lead to broader questions of policy coordination and coherence. In other words, whatever happens in terms of liberalization and digitalization, and even in terms of automatization (for example, self-driving cars and buses), will have to be considered from a broader public policy perspective, combining economic, social, and ecological considerations. In this sense, the regulation of urban mobility systems will serve as a laboratory of what is in store for the future of infrastructures more generally. But more about that in the concluding chapter of this book.

In this section on urban public transport, I have only discussed passenger transport. However, very similar considerations can be made for the transport of goods, something for which the term "city logistics" has been coined. The transport of goods in urban areas will indeed be affected in exactly the same way by urbanization, digitalization, and automatization and will ultimately be regulated very similarly to passenger mobility; that is, also from a combined economic, ecological, and perhaps even social point of view.

Other transport network industries

Unlike railways, road transport has always been unbundled, with vehicles – trucks, most buses, and cars – privately owned while the roads are public property. Only more recently, mainly as part of a process to develop road infrastructures, especially in emerging countries, have we witnessed the emergence of private toll roads, as well as privately owned and operated bridges and tunnels. How these infrastructures are "regulated" (by contract) has been discussed extensively in Chapter 6. Such unbundling is essentially made possible because hardly any interoperability issues exist between the infrastructure and the vehicles. Also, vehicles are globally standardized. Interoperability issues are only just about to emerge as a result of automatization and digitalization – the so-called intelligent transportation system (ITS) – an evolution that, without doubt, will trigger the regulation of road transport as well.

As for the transportation part, regulation of both trucks and buses (and even cars) exists in terms of both the environment (noise, pollution) and safety. However, little to no economic regulation exists, as competition in trucking and in busing seems to work. Still, regulation of road transport will only increase with growing congestion and pollution, digitalization, and intermodal competition; for example, between private, long-distance buses and rail. Policy makers will also become more active because of the financing needs of road maintenance and road development.

Maritime transport is somewhat comparable to air transport but without maritime traffic control: ships basically talk to each other and coordinate themselves on the high seas. Also, unlike in the air transport industry, self-regulation occurs. But just like in air transport (ICAO, created 1947), postal services (UPU, created 1872), and telecommunications (ITU, created 1864), an International Maritime Organization (IMO, created 1958) exists whose regulatory role exclusively pertains to safety and pollution but not to economic regulation. One other particularity in maritime transport pertains to so-called port-of-registry politics, where countries of registry compete against each other globally, leading to a race to the bottom in terms of standards and working conditions, in a much more exacerbated manner than is the case in trucking.

In economic terms, maritime transport displays strong network effects, just like all the other network industries. It also has some economies of scale, as ships, at least until recently, seemed to get bigger and bigger. However, the economies of scale are somewhat tempered by the fact that high sea shipping is dedicated: oil tankers are a totally different business from liquid natural gas tankers or container ships in terms of the ship and the ports they are using.

The only element of the maritime value chain that is somewhat regulated is ports. Like airports, maritime ports typically belong to local or regional authorities and sometimes to national governments. Yet liberalization, the unbundling of port activities, is typically less advanced than in the case of airports. Still, the regulatory issues are more or less similar, namely the questions of port charges and of port slot allocation. Unlike in the case of airports, big issues exist in terms of interconnection and interoperability between ships on the one hand and trucks, trains, and pipelines on the other hand. Corresponding regulatory policies are only recently emerging, handled as they were in the past by the industry itself.

Challenges for the maritime shipping industry are quite similar to those of the other transport sectors and pertain to automatization and subsequent considerations about safety, to digitalization, to market concentration (not the least triggered by the emergence of digital maritime shipping platforms), and to climate change and pollution of the high seas.

Conclusion: from transport to mobility

This chapter discussed separately the various transport modes, their liberalization, and their regulation. However, in the case of urban mobility and of city logistics, we clearly saw how most of these transport modes become increasingly integrated into a single transport or mobility chain, both for passengers and for goods. This evolution is driven simultaneously by digitalization, which allows for a much more coordinated approach, and by growing public policy concerns aimed at increasing economic and ecological efficiency. Transport as a whole is at the forefront of the type of considerations that, in my mind, will determine the future of the infrastructures. I will come back to this point in the concluding chapter of this book.

9   Energy

In this chapter, I discuss the network industries in the energy sector. I focus on electricity, at least when it comes to liberalization and regulation. I will therefore discuss gas only as it is treated differently from electricity. However, in Europe, gas liberalization originally advanced more rapidly than electricity liberalization, owing mainly to the reluctance of the vertically integrated national public electricity monopolies to liberalize.

Electricity

Electricity, like telecommunications and railways, emerged from the bottom up and from the private sector: private local generation plants and distribution networks (at low voltage levels) were developed in urban areas and were gradually connected to one another, leading over time to a more stable electricity supply. With the active involvement of nation-states in infrastructure development in the late 19th and early 20th centuries, electricity generation and distribution became nationalized; with such nationalization, high-voltage transmission grids were built. At the end of this process, one single, national, publicly owned and vertically integrated electricity company emerged in centralized countries. Federalist countries followed the same process, yet vertically integrated public monopolies mostly remained at the state (US) or regional (Germany, for example) level. (In some countries, local utilities still keep a monopoly over electricity distribution.) Governments subsequently invested in big electricity generation plants that typically used fossil fuels, mostly coal. In the rare countries with appropriate water resources, governments also invested in dams. After the Second World War, some governments invested heavily in nuclear power plants (United States, Russia, Japan, France, United Kingdom, Germany, and many other European countries). Electricity was considered absolutely foundational for national economic and social development.

The original value chain of the electricity sector reflects this national monopolistic structure: electricity is typically generated in a few big power plants (far away from where it is consumed) from which it is transmitted through the high-voltage grid across the country and then transformed to lower voltage levels and distributed to two types of customer: households and industries. Generation, transmission, transformation, and distribution are done within the same national or, at times, regional monopoly. These monopolies are somewhat interconnected – especially if they are regional monopolies inside a country or Europe – and by being so they help each other stabilize (or balance) the system. Since no competition exists among these companies, collaboration is no problem, and industry self-regulation has prevailed in the past.

There are sound economic reasons for electricity to be organized in this monopolistic way, as electricity generation, transmission, and distribution display huge economies of scale. Economies of density also exist, especially in urban areas. Finally, so-called economies of system stem from the fact that a vertically integrated monopoly can most efficiently balance the system; one particular physical characteristic of electricity that determines much of the operations is that electricity cannot be stored and must constantly be balanced. In other words, there must always be as much electricity produced as there is being consumed: thus, the larger the balancing area, the cheaper the costs of stabilizing the system. Finally, the original structure of electricity generation has led to heavy investments in generation plants that, at least at that time, only governments could afford. As for nuclear power plants, only governments would be willing and able to carry the economic risks.

Risk also explains, at least in part, the political characteristics of the electricity sector worldwide: not only are heavy investments needed for generation and high-voltage transmission lines, but the authorizations for these big generation plants and transmission lines naturally require heavy government involvement. As an example, civil society protested against nuclear power plants during the 1960s and 1970s and again after the accidents of Chernobyl (1986) and Fukushima (2014). But the sector is also politicized because of concerns about the security of supply (a country cannot afford a blackout or systemic lack of power) and because of the often cross-subsidized distribution tariffs for households (from industrial customers).

Liberalization

In terms of liberalization, there is again a US and an EU approach. The US approach, at least during the 1970s, was a half-hearted liberalization, in that vertically integrated electricity companies were forced by law to buy electricity from so-called independent power producers (IPPs) at a regulated price. This highly interventionist liberalization triggered private investment in generation plants across the country but left the rest of the sector, especially distribution, in the hands of local monopolists that were and continue to be regulated by the public utilities commissions. It also created the need to somewhat regulate interstate transmission, which in turn led to the creation of a federal electricity regulator – the Federal Energy Regulatory Commission (FERC) – which now exists alongside the utilities regulators at the state level.

The European approach to electricity liberalization was much more radical and less convoluted, at least in its early stages. The European Commission's (EC's) ambition was to create one single internal European electricity market, whereby any consumer – big or small – should be able to buy electricity produced anywhere in Europe and transmitted via what the EC called a "copper plate Europe," a frictionless European high-voltage grid. Like in the other network industries, the EC's basic idea is one of unbundling from the high-voltage transmission level all the way down to the distribution level. In short, generators should no longer own assets in transmission and consumers should be able to buy their electricity from sources other than their local distributor, such as generators, retailers, wholesalers, or other intermediaries, something called retail competition. Transmission and distribution companies should transport the electricity in a non-discriminatory manner, just like air traffic control guides airplanes. This new liberalized system leads directly to electricity trading and the corresponding emergence of electricity exchanges, regulated much like financial trading. This European approach, which has been successfully implement in Europe, is now in the process of being copied, including by many emerging countries such as China and Turkey.

Regulation

While this EU approach to electricity market liberalization is intellectually very appealing and basically leads to electricity becoming a commodity, it requires numerous and strong regulations to function. Indeed, the electricity system, even if Europeanized, will never work like a market: transmission and distribution will always remain monopolistic, generators will often have dominant positions, and consumers will sometimes need to be protected. Electricity trading poses problems of market integrity, and investments into long-lasting generation and transmission assets do not always seem to work. Finally, competition even among generators will always be limited by considerations of transmission, and system adequacy and grids will always cause technical barriers to trade, no matter how much one invests in removing bottlenecks. In short, this EU model of electricity market liberalization has given rise to a huge apparatus of regulation, and, so far, no end is in sight. But let us examine this electricity regulation step by step.

The major part of electricity regulation pertains to the grid and disproportionately to the high-voltage grid: generators should benefit from non-discriminatory access to the grid; that is, transmission and distribution. Grid tariffs not only have to be non-discriminatory but should also reflect the costs of an efficient and safe grid. Typically, this regulation is still done in a cost+ manner. Second, balancing costs are part of the grid tariff, and regulators must watch that energy balance is procured in an efficient and non-discriminatory manner, especially when generators and transmission operators are not perfectly unbundled (d'Arcy and Finger, 2014). Third, despite all grid investment, grid bottlenecks remain, which can lead to congestion rents; this requires subsequent congestion regulation. Typically, scarce grid capacity is auctioned off, and the regulator must ensure that auctions are non-discriminatory and especially that the proceeds of the auctions are reinvested into removing the bottlenecks. Fourth, regulation is needed in terms of accessibility to the grid by both generators and consumers and in terms of reasonable costs. Finally, the regulator must supervise the transmission (and to a lesser extent the distribution) operator so that investments are made in transmission adequacy. In other words, the grid requires truly heavy-handed regulation.

But this is not all: many electricity companies are still not totally unbundled at the transmission level and even more so at the distribution level. As a consequence, economic regulators also must ensure that such imperfect unbundling does not lead to market distortions; that is, unfair competitive advantages of the integrated companies over the new entrants. Furthermore, a totally new field of regulation is emerging to ensure market integrity via electricity- and more generally energy-trading regulation. Partially unbundled companies especially can benefit from insider knowledge and subsequent competitive advantages.

Future challenges

Many challenges await the not yet totally liberalized electricity sector, not only in Europe: technological changes in various areas, climate change, security of supply, and digitalization. All these challenges have the potential to slow down the process of liberalization, complexify regulation, and potentially stall if not revert the electricity liberalization process.

- Liberalization of the network industries was an exclusively institutional change, with technology assumed to be stable. This assumption did not hold in telecom, as we saw; we now see that it does not hold in the electricity sector, either. The first big technological changes happened on the generation side with substantial progress made in wind and especially solar electricity generation. Especially the latter led and continues to lead to much decentralized generation, contrary to the way the entire electricity grid was originally constructed and continues to be structured. Consequently, decentralized generation requires substantial investments in grid reinforcements. It also brings new challenges to balancing the electricity system with ensuing higher grid operating costs. But technological innovation does not stop at the generation level: smart metering and more recently battery and storage technologies challenge the very idea of unbundling, as these technologies force a much closer integration between generation and the grid, and ultimately question the very idea of liberalization by way of unbundling.

- Progress in these technologies has come about because of growing concern about climate change and the need to decarbonize energy production. In some countries, and after the Fukushima accident, a political will existed to phase out nuclear production (for example, Germany, Switzerland). Renewables and energy efficiency measures were seen as an alternative and promoted with heavy subsidies, thus distorting the market.
- Such market distortions, along with the lack of investment in generation, led to growing political concern about security of supply. Many European countries started to develop capacity reservation mechanisms, thus further distorting the already less than perfect European electricity market. And this evolution is likely to continue.
- And finally, digitalization provides the potential of peer-to-peer electricity trading as well as much more comprehensive energy services, just like in the case of mobility. This digitalization will further transform the electricity sector and will require an evolution in the way electricity and other infrastructures will have to be regulated in the future. I will discuss this in more detail in Chapter 11.

Gas

Both in terms of liberalization and in terms of re-regulation, the gas sector is very similar to the electricity sector. Gas liberalization is linked with electricity liberalization, as a more liberalized gas market will help generate more electricity from gas and by doing so produce some of the flexibilities needed to remedy volatile renewables. Gas-fired power plants also have the potential to replace coal-fired and nuclear power plants.

However, two big differences exist between electricity and gas. Both affect liberalization and regulation. The first is that, unlike electricity, gas is produced by very few countries. In the case of Europe, all gas producers are located outside of the EU (for example, Norway, Russia, and Algeria). This fact has significant implications for security of supply. In other words, gas is even more politicized than electricity.

The second difference pertains to the transmission grid: gas can be stored in dedicated storage facilities and even, to a certain extent, inside the grid. Balancing supply and demand is thus a much less important issue. However, regulators in the gas sector have to pay particular attention to the regulation of the corresponding storage facilities and especially to the question of non-discriminatory access to them. However, in all other areas – such as access to and pricing of the grid, unbundling, and trading – gas regulation is very similar if not identical to the regulation of the electricity sector.

10 Water

If air and maritime transport are the most global network industries, water, perhaps along with urban public transport, is certainly the most local one. It is also the least liberalized one, at least when it comes to access competition, as it has proven to be technically impossible. Except for some countries – for example, France and the United Kingdom – water is firmly in public hands, even though things have started to change as of late thanks to the spreading of the French model (public-private partnerships or PPPs). Typically, drinking and wastewater services are provided by local public water utilities, which come in different forms: separately, one drinking and one wastewater utility; integrated; or as part of a larger urban utility that includes electricity, gas, waste management, cable TV, and others.

The water value chain will structure this chapter: water is "abstracted," typically from groundwater, then pumped and cleaned in a local station; it is then transported and distributed to the end users or consumers. On a global scale, roughly 80 percent of abstracted water is used for agriculture (irrigation), 10 percent for industrial purposes, and 10 percent for household consumption. Water is generally not transported over long distances, as transportation costs are prohibitive. Once consumed, industrial and household water is collected (hopefully), transported to a cleaning station, cleaned (to a certain degree), and released into the groundwater, usually close to the water treatment plant because of the transportation costs. In this way, the "water cycle" is somewhat closed; however, if the released wastewater is still polluted, initial cleaning costs will be higher, at least for any downstream water utility.

From an economic point of view, both drinking and wastewater are typical network industries displaying important economies of scale and density. Water pipes have a lifetime of up to 80 years; putting them into the ground and replacing them (that is, digging up the streets) is extremely costly, to the point that it is economically more efficient to accept leakages (sometimes up to 40 percent for drinking water) before replacing the pipes. Water cleaning and water treatment are the other big cost factor: with growing pollution of groundwater and with ever more contaminated wastewater due to more chemicals and other polluting agents, cleaning and treatment costs are rising; technical expertise becomes ever more necessary. Historically, water is little regulated, at least from an economic point of view, except in the United States where public utilities commissions have long regulated water, mostly as a toll good.

Another characteristic of water is that the quality of both drinking water and wastewater is a public health concern; therefore, water is heavily regulated in terms of chemical and bacterial pollution. Water is a public service, and some consider water to be a "human right"; consequently, water must be accessible and affordable to all. Many regulations worldwide pertain to water affordability, accessibility, and equity. Finally, ever more regions of the world display water scarcity, owing to increasing consumption rates, high pollution, and drought. All this leads to the fact that water, especially drinking water, is highly politicized.

Liberalization

Liberalization of the water sector – both drinking water and wastewater – takes the form of competition for the market, franchising, and PPPs (Finger and Allouche, 2002). Water is actually where PPPs started in France, where historically 80 percent of the municipalities franchise their drinking water provision and their wastewater treatment to private operators. The typical PPP in the water sector is a lease contract of approximately 11 years in duration. Recall that in a lease contract, the franchisee makes some investments and collects the proceeds from the customers, among other agreements. Sometimes, both drinking water and wastewater are tendered together in one single lease contract.

Of course, such contracts are highly sophisticated as they "regulate" many things at the same time. The most important ones are water tariffs for the end users. These tariffs can simply reflect the fact of consumption or vary depending on the amount consumed. In some social tariffs, the price of the water increases (contrary to market logic) with increased consumption, the purpose being to discourage high consumption in scarce water areas and offer low-cost water services to poor households. Sometimes, the cost of treating the water is included in the drinking water tariff, as the amount of treated water is in principle identical to the amount of water consumed.

Moreover, such contracts also "regulate" price increases, either along a cost+ or a price-cap or even an incentive model, the goal always being to incentivize the franchisee to become more efficient. A typical water lease contract also "regulates" grid development and investments: it determines where the franchisee has to extend the network; for example, in new areas being developed by the municipality. Finally, a typical lease contract "regulates" maintenance of the water pipes (for example, leakage rates), the cleaning station, and the wastewater treatment station. The goal is to make sure that when the lease contract ends, the water infrastructures return to the municipality in the same condition as initially. Not only are all these "regulations" difficult to verify, owing to the asymmetry of information between the franchisee and the municipality, but the power relations typically favor the franchisee.

Regulation

As said, water is typically "regulated" by contract between the municipality and the franchisee. These contracts are highly sophisticated, but an unequal power relationship exists between the big multinational water companies and the municipalities (for example, asymmetry of information). Some academics have called for a national water regulator who, at the very least, could scrutinize the contracts and intervene and perhaps even cancel abusive contracts.

In the US approach, the situation is somewhat better, as water tariffs (called "rates") – but not contracts – are regulated by the public utilities commissions or public services commissions at the state level. Yet that approach is not satisfactory either, considering that the tendering process is beyond the scope of the regulators. In any case, much national regulation exists, this time in matters of public health and drinking water standards, as well as in terms of pollution and wastewater discharge standards.

The United Kingdom is an odd case, with water utilities privatized during the 1980s. This has led to very strong and powerful water regulation and regulators, not only in public health and pollution but also in economic terms. The EU has not yet taken up economic water regulation.

The water cycle and river-basin management

"River basin management," another French invention, was taken up by the EU in its 2000 Water Framework Directive. In this directive, the French approach to managing river basins was generalized to the main European river basins. A "river basin" is a catchment area and reflects an ecologically defined geographical area (for example, the Rhine river basin, the Rhone river basin, the Danube river basin). River basins typically cut across many countries. The idea of managing a river basin combines economics with ecology: downstream water utilities have to clean the water more if upstream water is discharged without sufficient cleaning. Consequently, upstream polluters should either clean their wastewater before discharging or pay downstream utilities to do so, a typical "polluter pays" approach and quite an effective one.

Future challenges

Future challenges for the water sector – drinking water, wastewater, and river basin management combined – do not pertain to liberalization. Rather, they result from global warming and ever higher groundwater pollution levels and relate mainly to water scarcity and thus to the question of the "optimal" allocation of the water resources. These challenges have an economic dimension, as it is possible and probably even desirable to price water resources according to scarcity. Yet a public service and even human rights dimension persists, given that it is difficult to cut off poor, non-paying households.

Also, in industrialized countries, water infrastructures are nearing the ends of their lifecycles. Heavy investments will be needed, money that the local public authorities typically do not have since they never priced the renewal of the infrastructures into the tariffs. Consequently, PPPs appear to be the only viable option for infrastructure renewal, not to mention for the development of new infrastructures in emerging and developing countries. In addition, ever higher pollution levels require ever more sophisticated cleaning technologies, which most of the medium and small municipalities do not have and cannot afford.

Consequently, it is likely that private water companies, operating along a PPP model, will only grow in the future. Given the economics of the water sector, this situation could easily lead to some sort of global water cartel, just like in many other network industries, where a few global logistics firms (for example, DHL, UPS), telecom operators (for example, Vodaphone, Orange, T-Telekom), airline alliances (for example, Star Alliance, Oneworld, Skyteam), or maritime shipping companies (Maersk, MSC) exploit both network effects and economies of scale, now at a global level. As we will see in the next chapter, this dynamic is even more pronounced when it comes to digitalization and digital platforms (Amazon, Alibaba, Airbnb, for example), which may well become the next new network industries.

11   New digital infrastructures

Having presented the traditional, classical, or typical infrastructures, I now turn to new or digital infrastructures. This chapter differs from the previous ones. I use the word "infrastructure" by analogy. Yet I will show that digital platforms do have the potential to become new infrastructures and that they should probably be regulated as such. My main argument is based on economics, namely on network effects and sunk costs. Economic reasons are also the main reasons why digital infrastructures should be regulated in the future, although, as in the other network industries, social and political arguments for such regulation also exist.

This chapter is structured as follows: in the first section, I show how liberalization has at least in part favored digitalization. In the second section, I explain how digitalization works and what digital platforms are. In the third section, I explain the economics of digital platforms and how the economics make them comparable to traditional infrastructures. The fourth section looks at the emergence of digital platforms in the traditional infrastructures, with the example of mobility. In the last section, I argue for the regulation of digital platforms.

From liberalization to digitalization

Almost everything written about network industries predates digitalization. In this book, I have mostly discussed the liberalization and re-regulation of the network industries as conceived before digitalization. In this section, I will show how the liberalization of these network industries actually prepared the ground for digitalization.

Digitalization as disruption

Recall that the initial view on the liberalization of the network industries was quite simplistic when it came to how markets were going to unfold and naïve when it came to technology. The effect on markets was not much of a problem: economic regulation rapidly developed to remedy market imperfections or even to substitute for markets that would never work perfectly. As for technology, the problem is more serious, as the promoters of liberalization and regulation did not anticipate technological change or think about how technology could affect liberalization and regulation. These promoters were mostly economists and politicians, not engineers.

But technology did evolve, and, to a certain extent, it evolved because of liberalization. Such evolution could have been anticipated: indeed, liberalization was supposed to and does actually lead to competition, which in turn leads to industry dynamics, as firms have to become more innovative. And innovation includes, but is not limited to, technological innovation. In the case of the electricity industry, I have given very concrete examples of how technological innovation in both generation (wind, solar) and the interfaces (metering, batteries) has dynamized the industry. Similar, but perhaps not as spectacular, technological innovations triggered or at least accelerated by liberalization are observed in the liberalized postal sector (for example, tracking and sorting technologies), in the telecommunications industry (being up to 5G, among others), on the road (for example, self-driving vehicles, electric vehicles), in the water sector (membrane technologies for water cleaning, for example), and in air transport (for example, drones).

But all these technological innovations are relatively minor compared to digitalization. And many are actually only possible because of digitalization, such as smart meters and self-driving vehicles. Digitalization as a technological (r)evolution is so massive for two reasons: first, digitalization is a pervasive technology in the sense that it permeates all other technologies and accelerates their innovation dynamics. Consequently, digitalization affects and transforms all network industries – and all industries for that matter.

The second reason why digitalization is so pervasive pertains to the fact that it affects and transforms the coordination among actors; that is, the economic, the social, and the organizational dimensions of everyday life. And, as we will see, liberalization – both because of unbundling and because of competition – has fragmented the network industries, thus creating an increased need for their coordination. This fragmentation has opened the door to digitalization, at least in the case of the network industries.

Conceptualizing network industry dynamics

The liberalization of the different network industries has dynamics to it, something that has drawn little attention in the literature so far but which, in the age of digitalization, can no longer be ignored. Such dynamics are best conceptualized in terms of a coevolution between institutional and technological change (Finger, Künneke and Groenewegen, 2005). As mentioned, liberalization was primarily an institutional change that had to be accompanied immediately by re-regulation, another exclusively institutional change. But things did not stop there: liberalization triggered industry dynamics – growing competition and market creation – a concept captured in the figure below by the space created between institutions and technology. Institutions and technology constitute the limits of how far the market can develop. In other words, as liberalization (institutions, rules) and technology evolve, the institutional and technological boundaries to the markets recede. Digitalization now appears to be yet another technological innovation that expands the market potential in the various network industries. Figure 11.1 summarizes this conceptualization of network industry dynamics.

But there is more: liberalization, especially EU-style liberalization with unbundling and many new actors that have to be coordinated, leads to new interfaces, and regulation becomes the privileged means to coordinate these interfaces. As institutional economics teaches us, coordination has a cost, and a growing coordination need generates growing costs (so-called transaction costs). Not astonishingly then, many new technologies emerge where coordination cost savings can be made. In other words, new technologies are at least a partial answer to the problems of coordination as created by liberalization. And digitalization is precisely one of these interface technologies that has the potential to significantly reduce coordination costs.

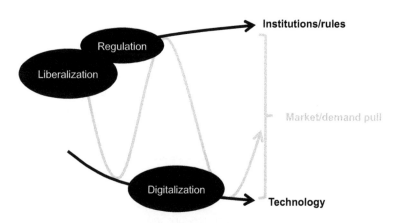

Figure 11.1 Coevolution between technology and institutions

From digitalization to digital platforms

Before showing how digitalization can reduce transaction costs, let us discuss what digitalization is all about:

- *Data generation and storage:* Thanks to technological innovation, data can now be generated by more and more devices – sensors, radio-frequency identification tags, cameras, near-field communication and smartphones – and by more and more actors, such as telecommunications operators, credit card companies, banks, public administration, hospitals, and users themselves. Such data can be generated at ever lower costs and in ever bigger numbers. The same goes for storage and retrieval: data storage requires ever smaller space in ever smaller devices. The costs of storing and retrieving data are also decreasing rapidly.
- *Data exchange:* Again thanks to technological innovation, ever more data can be exchanged ever more rapidly at an ever lower cost over ever bigger distances – basically globally. Three layers of such data exchange exist: the most basic layer is the telecommunications infrastructure, be it mobile telephony or fiber. The second layer is the Internet, the connection of the telecommunications infrastructure to the various devices, be it computers, cell phones, cars, or fridges (the "Internet of things"). Ever more users and devices are being connected via the global Internet. The third layer is the worldwide web: thanks to standardized protocols, data can be exchanged among senders and receivers in ever bigger numbers and more and more in real time.
- *Data analytics:* All the above remains useless if data is not analyzed. Only after analysis does data become valuable information. Significant technological developments have occurred here: algorithms and, increasingly, artificial intelligence software are able to learn from past mistakes and to improve. Ever bigger amounts of data – "big data" – can be analyzed and visually displayed ever more rapidly in ever more sophisticated manners, algorithms being at the heart of the matter.

What we today call "digital platforms" are basically algorithms capable of analyzing and visualizing these data. Digital platforms are thus software and software companies that collect data and analyze them using sophisticated algorithms, which includes "curating" or "cleaning" the data. Data curation mainly means annotating the data and generating metadata to make links and determine which data are of value.

The economics of digital platforms

Digital platforms are clearly not traditional, physical infrastructures. We use the word infrastructure mainly because digital platforms display the same two main economic characteristics as traditional infrastructures: network effects and sunk costs (economies of scale).

From direct to indirect network effects

Throughout this book, I have shown that network industries are economically characterized by strong network effects: the more users connected to the network, the better for all other customers. Network effects lead to monopolization. In the traditional network industries, such monopolization was mainly effective at the national level because political boundaries and issues of interconnection and interoperability prevented the monopoly from reaching beyond national borders. These "direct network effects" also operate with digital platforms, such as the Apple store, eBay, booking.com, or Airbnb. To take one example, the more hotels that can be found on booking.com, the more booking.com will be attractive to users, which in turn makes booking.com more attractive to the hotels, and on and on. Digital platforms thus display very powerful dynamics toward monopolization, but this time a global monopolization without any national borders, a situation that has become "winner takes all."

In addition to direct network effects, digital platforms display "indirect network effects." Indirect network effects were identified by Rochet and Tirole (Rochet and Tirole, 2003) back in 2003 as operating in free newspapers, payment cards, gaming consoles, and more before the emergence of digital platforms. Whereas direct network effects reflect two-sided markets, indirect network effects operate in three- or even multi-sided markets. Let us take the example of free (non-paying) newspapers. The direct network effects in traditional newspapers pertain to the fact that the more readers there are, the better the editorial content (quality) of the journal, which in turn attracts more readers. Indirect network effects stem from a third party: the more readers there are, the more advertisers find the newspaper attractive. More advertising, in turn, reduces the price of the newspaper to the readers, which in turn increases the number of readers. These same indirect network effects operate in all digital platforms, as advertisers typically become the third party to the multi-sided market.

Amazon is a typical example of a multi-sided market: The more items on the platform, the more customers will be attracted to it. The more customers on the platform, the more attractive it is to sellers. The more buyers and sellers on the platform, the more attractive Amazon becomes to advertisers.

The more advertisers that use Amazon, the cheaper the items can be sold, thus making the platform even more attractive to both customers and sellers. In the case of Amazon, one even finds a fourth party to the market, namely shippers: the more items shipped through Amazon, the more attractive Amazon becomes to shippers (because of their own economies of scale and density); the cheaper the shipping, the more attractive the platform becomes for sellers, buyers, and advertisers. These indirect network effects are very powerful, much more powerful than the direct network effects, and therefore they exacerbate the winner-takes-all dynamics.

Sunk costs

As in traditional network industries, digital platforms have sunk costs leading to economies of scale. Whereas in the traditional network industries, the investments were mainly "sunk" into physical infrastructures such as water pipes, rail tracks, high-voltage electricity grids, or gas pipelines, the upfront investments are mainly into two things in the case of digital platforms: the development of algorithms and the acquisition of users to unlock – "ignite" is the term often used – the platform. Igniting the platform happens by giving discounts to customers, subsidizing the providers of the services, or both. One can debate whether algorithms constitute sunk costs, as they are developed in parallel to the growth of the platform, but they are certainly the platform's unique competitive advantage.

Digital platforms in the traditional network industries

Digital platforms in the traditional network industries are in their infancy. So far, concrete examples exist only in transport or mobility and, to a lesser extent, in energy. This section presents the case of mobility and then derives the possible impacts of digitalization on the traditional infrastructures in general. These impacts will serve as a basis for considerations about regulating digital platforms in the next section (Montero and Finger, 2017).

From separate transport modes to Mobility-as-a-Service (MaaS)

Mobility-as-a-Service (MaaS) is the perfect example of how digital platforms enter the infrastructure and impact them. MaaS has overtaken the transport sector. I anticipate that similar developments will occur, sooner or later, in all other network industries, even though MaaS may be somewhat extreme and therefore an excellent case to study.

The entry point for digital platforms into any network industry is its fragmentation and the need to coordinate the infrastructure systems.

Network industries are, as I have argued all along in this book, complex socio-technical systems that can function only as systems, with coordination among the different parts of the system. Liberalization – and especially EU-style liberalization based on unbundling – cannot and does not change this technological reality but makes it more complex by increasing the need for coordination. This growing fragmentation also explains, in part, the need for regulation in the different network industries in the past. But digital platforms replace some of these coordination functions, only to lead to the need for regulating the digital platforms later on (see next section).

In the case of transport, the different modes have been liberalized separately from one another (see Chapter 8). Liberalization has taken place either by unbundling (for example, rail) or by franchising and PPPs (for example, urban public transport modes). Thus, transport today is a highly fragmented network industry. This fragmentation is a problem for customers who want only to move from A to B, especially in the urban context where cars are no longer a viable option as they have become too cumbersome.

Digital mobility platforms – so-called MaaS platforms – become the new digital interfaces between the traditional transport service providers and the customers, offering an integrated mobility solution (from A to B) to customers by coordinating the various transport modes into one single seamless journey with a single ticket. Figure 11.2 illustrates this evolution.

In the same way that Amazon coordinates between a seller and a buyer, Airbnb coordinates between the owner of an apartment and a renter, or Uber coordinates between a driver and a traveler, the MaaS platform coordinates between the supplier of a transport offer (which can even include Uber) and the customer. The more fragmented the offer, the more important the role of the coordinator; that is, the bigger the value added for the customer. And here is precisely where the power of digital platforms lies.

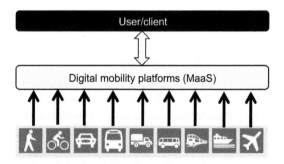

Figure 11.2 From transport modes to MaaS

Mobility as it is currently organized is highly inefficient due to its fragmented nature. Traditional ways of coordinating among these transport modes are expensive if not impossible. Digital mobility platforms coordinate these various transport offers for the customers. Network effects apply in the sense that the more transport offers coordinated by the MaaS platform, the more attractive the platform becomes for the customer; inversely, the more customers using the platform, the more attractive the platform becomes for the various transport service providers.

The MaaS platform does not add any value to the transport services per se; passengers still sit in a taxi or ride on a train or metro. The real value added is the reduction in the costs of coordination and the corresponding efficiency gains: travelling across transport modes becomes less time consuming, as the modes are better coordinated among themselves and especially as the customers do not have to coordinate by themselves.

To summarize, the more fragmented a network industry – and liberalization and unbundling have further contributed to such fragmentation – the more likely digital platforms will, sooner or later, move into that network industry. But a business case must exist: the customer must be better off than when he or she had to coordinate the different infrastructure services by him- or herself, thanks to the platform, or the transport service providers must receive more customers to better use their assets.

Main impacts of digital platforms on the network industries

Digital platforms will impact the network industries' infrastructures. Again, transport can be taken as a highly illustrative case, even though the considerations are valid more generally.

- As Figure 11.2 shows, with the emergence of digital platforms, users of public transport become customers of the platform and no longer of the transport service providers. Consequently, the platform ends up having much more knowledge of the customers than any of the transport service providers. The platform can then develop ever better and ever more personalized services, whereas the traditional transport service provider simply becomes a "mule" servicing the platform.
- This shift in customer ownership in turn has immediate consequences on the value added and profits. The platform takes a margin in between the infrastructure service provider and the customer, just as a credit card company takes a percent from the seller of the good (and often also from the buyer). While the underlying infrastructure provider can still make some profit, a portion of what was made previously now goes to the platform.

- Margins and profits for the underlying infrastructure providers are further decreased because platforms exacerbate intermodal competition. The platform can play the different service providers or transport modes against one another and thus further reduce their margins (while increasing the margins of the platform).
- Finally, digital platforms lead to a problem financing the infrastructures: not only are the margins of the traditional infrastructure providers reduced because of competition among themselves, but at least part of the profits has shifted to the platform. This money will be lacking when it's time to maintain the existing infrastructure or invest in the development of new infrastructures. As a consequence, either the quality of the traditional infrastructure services will decline, or the public sector will have to compensate, which amounts to a public subsidy to the private platforms.

In other words, in the medium and long term, digital platforms in the network industries will negatively affect the very sustainability of these infrastructures. This effect, and many other things, will sooner or later call for some sort of platform regulation. The main question will be how to regulate these digital platforms, and the answer will depend on how these digital platforms are seen: are they simply new competitive services, or are they a new type of infrastructure?

Regulating digital platforms

Digital platforms can be considered a new type of network industry. From an economic point of view, digital platforms display similar, yet even more powerful network effects than traditional network industries – not only direct effects but also indirect network effects. These network effects naturally lead to monopolization. Therefore, just like with the traditional network industries, digital platforms should be regulated, at least for their monopoly power.

However, digital platforms present more problems than the potential of abusing market power: problems of revenue sharing, equity among service providers, market distortion resulting from underlying algorithms, and more. The purpose here is not the give a full-fledged regulatory policy as to how to regulate digital platforms as the new network industries. This would be premature. Rather, I would like to indicate the main areas where such regulation of digital platforms in infrastructures will have to be considered in the future. Also, I will not discuss more classical and more general issues such as data security, privacy, data ownership, or access to data, which apply to all digital platforms including retail, health care, banking, and e-government platforms.

- Direct and especially indirect network effects in the case of digital platforms lead to monopolization. Once a digital platform is established in a given industry, it is very difficult, if not impossible, for another digital platform to enter the market. Unlike the traditional network industry operators, which were either national or local monopolies, the new digital platform monopolists are likely to be global or at least supra-national. Limiting their market power or trying to break them up will be difficult using traditional national competition law and may be possible only by the big powers – the United States, China, or the EU.
- "Net neutrality" is a concept borrowed from telecommunications regulation: it refers to the strategy of digital content providers preventing traditional telecommunications providers from privileging their own content over that of the one of the companies simply using the telecom infrastructure. In the age of digital platforms, the same argument can and must be used against digital platforms: digital platforms should be neutral vis-à-vis the infrastructure services they offer via their platform, and this "platform neutrality" should be enforced by the regulator. For example, a MaaS platform should not discriminate against certain transport operators and modes so that the user has the maximum choice of services and transparency as to the nature and the quality of the different services provided on the platform. Platform neutrality will be difficult to regulate, as the potential for discrimination lies within the algorithms at the core of the digital platform.
- Platform neutrality will lead – exactly as it did in the case of liberalizing the traditional network industries – to full institutional unbundling, not allowing digital platform operators to own any underlying physical infrastructure service providers.
- Platforms appropriate at least some of the value they generate from the underlying infrastructure services. The question arises as to whether the usage of this infrastructure is properly remunerated. In the case of the liberalization of the traditional infrastructures, the monopolistic infrastructures were typically regulated in a cost+ manner, and these costs were included in the price of the final service. For example, the price of electricity is composed of an energy price determined by the market and a tariff for the use of the grid, which is generally regulated by a cost+ method. Similar considerations should apply with digital platforms: at the very least, the prices platforms pay to the underlying infrastructure service providers – for example, the train operators – should be set such that they do not jeopardize the sustainability of the infrastructure in the long run. This is primarily a public policy concern, more precisely a security of supply concern. Thus, public policy must

regulate digital platforms to ensure that the underlying infrastructures are not "hollowed out" by the digital platforms.

- Additional public policy or public service concerns apply in the case of digital platforms, as they do with traditional network industries. For example, if digital platforms become the preferred if not exclusive way of providing infrastructure services – for example, MaaS, EaaS (Energy-as-a-Service), WaaS (Water-as-a-Service) – public service concerns will have to be addressed by regulation and will pertain to equity (equal treatment of similar types of customers), accessibility, and affordability of the services via the platforms. Public policy concerns will also exist in terms of ecological issues, for example, when governments promote electric modes of transport rather than fossil fuel-based ones, and platforms will have to incorporate such public policy (and public service) objectives into their algorithms.

The last question is where such regulation could or should occur. In the case of the winner-takes-all problem, global regulation is obviously needed, which furthermore must be based on competition law and competition regulation principles. But in the other four cases – net-neutrality, unbundling, revenue sharing, and public policy – regulation at a national level is still conceivable. In my opinion, such regulation can be sector-specific regulation, even though sectors will have to be broadened somewhat to cover all modes of mobility (MaaS), all modes of energy provision (EaaS), et cetera.

12 Conclusion

Figure 11.1 in the previous chapter illustrates the conceptualization of network industry evolution and dynamics that underlie this book. These dynamics have indeed started with their liberalization in the context of economic globalization during the late 1980s and early 1990s. In the beginning, this dynamic was triggered by their liberalization, a purely institutional transformation. Consequently, the main drivers of liberalization were exclusively institutional actors, namely national governments (UK, US), the EU, and multilateral organizations (World Bank, International Monetary Fund). In the network industries, such liberalization was accompanied by an additional layer of institutional actors in the form of independent regulatory authorities at the national and European levels. Two different approaches to liberalization – a US approach and an EU approach – leading to at least two, but in reality many more, institutional arrangements of regulating and governing the network industries, arrangements that are in themselves also dynamic.

Liberalization created, as expected and desired, some sort of market environment and engendered numerous new market players active in various segments of the different network industries. These new players forced the original actors – typically vertically integrated public monopolies that were mostly state-owned enterprises (SOEs) – to transform and innovate. In some of the network industries (for example, telecommunications) and in some of the countries (for example, the United Kingdom), these SOEs were privatized. Slowly, yet at varying speeds, the different infrastructure sectors indeed became network industries with all this entails, namely the creation of demand for network industry services and the subsequent business and strategic behavior of the market players involved.

And this is where technological dynamics comes in: as part of their strategic behavior, the market players in the different network industries turned to a technology strategy or more generally used technological innovation to further their business strategies, the new entrants more so than the incumbents, of course. Digitalization, which emerged in parallel to and outside of network industry dynamics, is now embraced by market players inside the network industries, accelerating and transforming the dynamics of network industry liberalization. As an immediate consequence, the boundaries between the different infrastructures are blurring. This blurring of boundaries requires the various institutional actors (for example, regulators, policy makers at the urban, national, and EU levels) to evolve as well. In this conclusion, I offer my thoughts as to how to look at the current evolution of the network industries, as well as at the challenges they will face in the not so distant future.

A layered approach

The evolution of the network industries over the past 100+ years can be described in a very simplified way as a process of emerging layers: these layers result both from institutional changes (liberalization, in the 1980s) and technological changes (digitalization, in 2010), as illustrated by Figure 12.1.

Prior to their liberalization, most of the network industries were, as we have seen, vertically integrated monopolies at the national level (rail, electricity, gas, postal services, telecommunications) or at the local level (water, wastewater, urban public transport), mostly operated by SOEs. Air transport was never vertically integrated, and airlines used to be national monopolies, as did air traffic control; airports were typically local monopolies. Maritime and road transport were never vertically integrated, either, and competition always existed among shippers and among trucks, buses, and cars. Ports are typically national or local monopolies, as are roads.

Liberalization as of the late 1980s, especially EU-style liberalization, tried to change this, mainly by unbundling. In unbundling's most simple

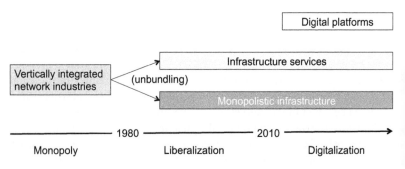

Figure 12.1 Network industry evolution

version – which never played out exactly as planned – network industries were divided up into monopolistic infrastructures (rail tracks, electricity grids, gas pipelines, fixed telephone lines, water and wastewater pipes, roads, and air traffic control) and competitive services on the basis of these infrastructures (for example, rail services, electricity and gas services, telecommunications services, postal services, water and wastewater services, urban public transport services, and air transport services). Unbundling results in a two-layered approach to the network industries, leading to a very complex way of regulating the different, now very fragmented network industries.

With digitalization a third layer emerges, the digital platforms. I have argued that we should conceptualize such digital platforms as new infrastructures. The two other layers will continue to be indispensable for the network industry services to be provided. For example, even if train trips (as part of a broader mobility package) are booked and bought via a digital platform, trains will have to be boarded physically and operated by train operating companies. The railway infrastructures will still be needed. However, it is still unclear what the emergence of this third layer means for network industry regulation.

Prior to liberalization, sector-specific, independent regulation in the different network industries did not exist. In the United States, public utilities commissions oversaw the rates of the local monopolies and still do. In the rest of the world, infrastructure monopolies were "regulated" by way of public ownership and in some countries and some sectors (for example, France) by way of contracts. With liberalization and unbundling, "regulation by ownership" became untenable, and "regulation by contract" and by state-level public utilities regulatory commissions (the US model) will become untenable as well. The job of developing an entirely new approach to regulating the liberalized and unbundled network industries has been taken on by the European Commission as of the 1990s, and I have devoted a substantial portion of this book to explaining it. In essence, this regulatory approach is based on an independent, sector-specific regulator that remedies the various market failures that persist even after liberalization or that, paradoxically, emerge as a result of it. However, the full-fledged version of liberalized network industries and a matching regulatory approach is not likely to occur, owing to emerging and increasingly overriding public policy concerns.

Raising public policy concerns

In the beginning, at least in Europe, regulatory intervention into the different network industries was only conceived as a means to facilitate the emergence and the perfection of infrastructure markets. Unlike in the United States, where regulation focused on local monopolies and tried to strike a balance between economic and social objectives, in Europe (and the rest of the world for that matter) the original ideas of regulation pertained to limiting the monopoly to the portion that is indispensable for competitors to operate (the so-called natural monopoly), to regulating this monopoly from a purely economic (efficiency) point of view, and to ensuring that competition would otherwise work. The situation never turned out that way for a variety of reasons, including initial intellectual flaws in liberalization thinking, strategic behavior of the incumbents, and public policy concerns that became ever more important, parallel with the unfolding of liberalization.

Public or universal services

The first public policy concern, public services, existed from the very beginning. Indeed, the European Commission had already anticipated it, as it was aware that markets generate inequities. But unlike the US approach, which incorporated public service concerns into its regulatory framework, the EU treated it separately and independently from purely economic regulation. This treatment led to separate public services or, as they became called, a universal services obligation regulation. The basic idea was to define a minimal service in terms of accessibility, affordability, and quality to which all consumers even in the liberalized network industries would have a right and which one of the operators in each network industry, typically the incumbent, had to provide. While intellectually sound, this approach nevertheless had a problem, inasmuch as the financing of these universal services was not solved, leading to financing and market distortion problems that the European Commission simply delegated to the nation-states. In the meantime, even more important public policy concerns arose.

Environment and climate

Environmental concerns (pollution) and climate change concerns (global warming) came to prominence around ten years after liberalization set in and have started to disrupt the liberalization and market regulation approach. So far, this disruption has mostly been in the energy sector, where some governments have started to promote and heavily subsidize renewable energies (for example, in Germany and Denmark), thus disrupting market signals. In reaction, other countries developed subsidy schemes to keep their not-so-renewable generation facilities running. Having no option other than to continue on its liberalization path, the EU is trying to fit all these subsidy schemes into a competition regulation framework; for example, by forcing subsidies to be tendered. However, this fix only further complexifies an already highly complex approach to network industry regulation. Energy serves here as an illustrative example of how other public policies interfere and sometimes even override the original liberalization agenda. This interference is likely to continue and accelerate as environmental and climate concerns penetrate all other network industries, beginning with transport and water but eventually moving even to digital platforms (for example, because of their voracious energy-consuming data centers).

Foundational economics and security of supply

Foundational economics and security of supply – as well as security more generally – will be the next public policy concerns disrupting or at least reorienting the liberalization and market regulation agenda. Security of supply concerns have emerged first in the energy sector, but broader foundational economic concerns are rapidly emerging in the different nation-states, mainly because liberalized infrastructure markets do not seem to create the investment incentives that are indispensable to develop or sometimes simply to maintain the infrastructures – energy, transport, water – in the long run. Governments are thus increasingly intervening by either setting these incentives or even investing themselves, thus adding to infrastructure market distortion. Also, national military security concerns have limited the liberalization agenda in numerous countries (for example, in regard to ports, air traffic control, energy).

Digitalization

The previous chapter examined emerging public policy concerns related to digitalization. Even though digitalization in general and digital platforms in particular are promoted by Silicon Valley as the new engine of liberalization, disillusionment, especially in the case of the network industries, may soon set in, owing to national sovereignty, security, privacy, and industrial policy concerns. Ensuing, mainly national regulation will further distort the original liberalization agenda, and perhaps ultimately stall it altogether, especially if digital platforms are considered as new, foundational infrastructures. In short, even though digitalization is being sold as a new impetus for further global economic liberalization and may be such an impetus that public policy concerns could well override this potential.

What future for the liberalizing network industries?

This leaves us with the question of whether liberalization of the network industries has come to a dead end. While liberalization was obviously both a reflection of and an active contribution to the overall economic globalization dynamics of the 1980s, economic globalization has led to profound concerns in terms of its social desirability and ecological viability. Network industries are directly affected by such concerns, as seen by the various public policy issues emerging. Independent, sector-specific, and technocratic economic regulation, after all, reflects policies and politics and will therefore not be sufficient to deal with these emerging public policy concerns. However, network industry regulation will not go away, as it has been too firmly institutionalized. On the contrary, it will be penetrated by these emerging public policy concerns and will merge them into an ever more complicated and complexifying regulatory approach to the various network industries, as well as increasingly across these industries.

While I am the first to criticize some of the original ideas about network industry liberalization as being naïve and even flawed to the extent that they have triggered sometimes heavy-handed regulation to remedy the flaws, a profound transformation of the network industries was long overdue. Indeed, the traditional model of providing infrastructure services via SOEs was simply no longer tenable in the context of globalization, and the liberalization of the network industries was a very welcome impetus to change this. Of course, the vertically integrated, former or current, state-owned monopolists did not welcome the process and delayed it wherever they could. Yet, to their credit, some of the warnings of these public enterprises against the consequences of liberalization turned out to be true, even though these same public enterprises did not have an answer to these warnings, either.

But the slowing down, stalling, or, in many cases, the perversion of the liberalization agenda in some of the network industries cannot be blamed solely on the incumbents (SOEs), most of which tried to operate in a liberalized environment while continuing to provide social or public services. If at all, it can be blamed on policy incoherence resulting from the naïve assumption that infrastructures could be turned into fully functioning markets thanks only to economic regulation.

Network industries existed before liberalization and will continue to exist after liberalization, just as they existed before and will continue to exist with digitalization. They will exist because increasingly complex and increasingly urbanized societies will need ever more infrastructures to function. These infrastructures will also need ever better governance to make them function.

References

Coll, S. (1988). *The Deal of the Century: The Break-Up of AT&T*. New York: Touchstone Books.

D'Arcy, A. and M. Finger (2014). The Challenges of Imperfectly Unbundled TSOs: Can Corporate Governance or Regulatory Action Mitigate Such Imperfection? *Competition and Regulation in Network Industries*, Vol. 15, No. 2, pp. 117–137.

Finger, M. and J. Allouche (2002). *Water Privatisation: Transnational Corporations and the Re-regulation of the Water Industry*. London: SPON Press.

Finger, M. and M. Auduoin (eds.) (2018). *The Governance of Smart Transportation Systems: New Organizational Structures for Mobility*. Berlin: Springer.

Finger, M. and K. Button (eds.) (2017). *Air Transport Liberalization: A Critical Assessment*. Cheltenham: Edward Elgar.

Finger, M. and C. Jaag (eds.) (2015). *The Routledge Companion on Network Industries*. London: Routledge.

Finger, M. and R. Künneke (eds.) (2011). *International Handbook of Network Industries: The Liberalization of Infrastructure*. Cheltenham: Edward Elgar.

Finger, M., Künneke, R. and J. Groenewegen (2005). The Quest for Coherence Between Institutions and Technologies in Infrastructures. *Journal of Network Industries*, Vol. 6, No. 4, pp. 227–260.

Finger, M. and P. Messulam (eds.) (2015). *Rail Economics, Regulation and Policy in Europe*. Cheltenham: Edward Elgar.

Foundational Economy Collective (2018). *Foundational Economy*. Manchester: Manchester University Press.

Knieps, G. (2014). *Network Economics: Principles, Strategies and Competition Policy*. Berlin: Springer.

Künneke, R. (2008). Institutional Reform and Technological Practice: The Case of Electricity. *Industrial and Corporate Change*, Vol. 17, No. 2, pp. 233–265.

Majone, G. (ed.) (2005). *Regulating Europe*. London: Routledge.

Ménard, C. (2000). *Institutions, Contracts and Organizations: Perspectives From New Institutional Economics*. Cheltenham: Edward Elgar.

Montero, J. and M. Finger (2017). Platformed! Network Industries and the New Digital Paradigm. *Competition and Regulation in Network Industries*, Vol. 18, Nos. 3&4, pp. 217–239.

Nicita, A. and F. Belloc (2016). *Liberalization in Network Industries: Economics, Policy and Politics*. Berlin: Springer.

Rochet, J.-C. and J. Tirole (2003). Platform Competition in Two-Sided Markets. *Journal of the European Economic Association*, Vol. 1, No. 4, pp. 990–1029.

Strouse, J. (1999). *Morgan: American Financier*. New York: Random House.

Glossary

APM	Award Penalty Mechanism
ATC	Air Traffic Control
ATM	Air Traffic Management
BRT	Bus Rapid Transit
CPI	Consumer Price Index
DG MOVE	Directorate General Mobility and Transport, European Commission
EC	European Commission
ERA	European Railway Agency
EU	European Union
FDI	Foreign Direct Investment
FERC	Federal Energy Regulatory Commission
FS	Ferrovie dello Stato
ICAO	International Civil Aviation Organization
ICT	Information and Communication Technology
IMF	International Monetary Fund
IMO	International Maritime Organization
IPP	Independent Power Producer
IRA	Independent Regulatory Authority
ITS	Intelligent Transportation Systems
ITU	International Telecommunications Union
KPI	Key Performance Indicator
LNG	Liquefied Natural Gas
MaaS	Mobility-as-a-Service
MRP	Multiyear Rate Plan
ORR	Office of Road and Rail (UK)
OTT	Over-the-Top
PBR	Performance-Based Regulation
PPP	Public Private Partnership
PTT	Post, Telegraph, Telecom

RAB	Regulatory Asset Base
RoR	Rate-of-Return (regulation)
RPI	Retail Price Index
SES	Single European Sky
SNCF	Société Nationale des Chemins de Fer Français
SOE	State-Owned Enterprise
TNC	Transnational Corporation
TOC	Train Operating Company
UAV	Unmanned Automated Vehicle
UPS	United Parcel Service
UPU	Universal Postal Union
US	United States
OSO	Universal Services Obligation
WACC	Weighted Average Cost of Capital
WB	World Bank

Index

For Product Safety Concerns and Information please contact our EU
representative GPSR@taylorandfrancis.com
Taylor & Francis Verlag GmbH, Kaufingerstraße 24, 80331 München, Germany